Reviews for *The*

MW00942981

"Having actually just met Carrie, I purchased her book because of her upbeat and enthusiastic presentations. The knowledge and thoughts one takes away after reading this book can be used in many situations. It is a must read for anyone in a leadership position. Buy it and you won't be sorry!"

–Jerry Zanni DDS

"I found this book just at the right time. It is a perfect book to use with my management team. I like how the main points are so simple but powerful. Also, I love how it engages the reader in thinking about what the concepts mean to them. I plan on using it as a training tool."

–James A. Ryan

"I found this book to be inspiring, informative and written with passion. The tools, the techniques, and strategies are universally applicable to any profession. Read it!"

–Dr. A. Rosen

"*The Dream Boss* is written by the vivacious, positively electric, Carrie Stack! Carrie has helped thousands with her inspirational talks around the country, and now she has put all her little gold nuggets into this powerful book. *The Dream Boss* is packed with strategies to create positive interactions and changes in yourself, and your staff. It's a quick read, made especially for busy professional, with no time. Five Stars! Highly Recommend! Buy another for YOUR Boss."

–Lisa Pelonzi

THE
DREAM BOSS

THE
DREAM BOSS

inspire individuals and teams to succeed

By Carrie Stack, M.Ed.

Say Yes Institute
121 Loring Avenue, Suite 250
Salem, MA 01970
(508) 527-7047
carrie@sayyesinstitute.com
www.sayyesinstitute.com

Ordering information:

Additional copies are available on *The Dream Boss* eStore: www.createspace.com/5403494, on Kindle, and other devices.

Special discounts are available on quantity purchases by corporations, associations, and others. For details, contact the Say Yes Institute at the address above.

Printed by CreateSpace, an Amazon.com Company

Cover photo by ©iStock.com/koratmember

Author photo by Lisa Pelonzi

Cover and book design by Lisa McKenna, Curious Marie, LLC

TO PBJ

You modeled and taught what it means to be a powerful, positive, and professional leader, helping so many of us become better at what we do and how we do it. Thank you for the impact you have had, and continue to have, on so many lives. It would be a better world if everyone had the privilege of starting a career with the experience of a "PBJ" kind of boss.

Inspire yourself and others will be inspired.

Motivate yourself and others will be motivated.

Develop yourself and others will start to develop themselves.

Be an example first and then the world changes around you.

–Author Unknown

Contents

> *Do not be concerned about others not appreciating you. Be concerned about your not appreciating others.*
>
> —CONFUCIUS

Acknowledgments

The acknowledgments section could be overwhelming because in my coaching, training, and consulting I have had the privilege of working with thousands and thousands of people around professional and personal growth. They have all contributed to the evolution of my work and this book is a direct extension of countless hours of the individual and group work I have done supporting people to build emotional intelligence skills.

I have come to understand all people, regardless of age, education, experience, position etc., are simply looking to live peaceful, happy, and fulfilling lives. People want to feel connected and valued, with the ability to positively contribute to the world around them. It is an amazing opportunity to share tools/strategies that could contribute to someone's life experience and I am grateful for the consistent willingness people have to try on new ways of thinking about their lives, experiences, perspectives, and relationships.

To past/ current clients:
Thank you for giving me the opportunity to cross paths with you on this journey, it has been an honor. To the individuals that have sat in my office for coaching, the groups of managers/supervisors I have provided coaching/training to, and all of the larger teams that I have trained, please know your energy, openness, and honesty as you explored new tools/

strategies is the reason that this book was written.

I have appreciated your ongoing feedback, both immediate as well as years later, about what worked and what you struggled with. Your input helped expand/develop these tools in order to ensure they are as useful as possible, to as many as possible.

Finally, thank you for your willingness to allow humor in to this equation. Thank you for the laughter, the openness to see imperfections, and for being open to trying new ways of being, in order to experience new ways of living. I couldn't do this work if there wasn't room to laugh, so thank you for giving me lots of space to find and share the humor!

And, to those that I have yet to have the pleasure of meeting:
It is my hope you found something useful in this book and you will be trying out some new skills/tools in your world. I look forward to the possibility of our paths crossing in the future because I'm going to need your insight and brilliance for the next book!

> *People travel to wonder at the height of the mountains,*
>
> *at the huge waves of the seas,*
>
> *at the long course of the rivers,*
>
> *at the vast compass of the ocean,*
>
> *at the circular motion of the stars,*
>
> *and yet, they pass by themselves without wondering.*

–St. Augustine

From the Author

I f you are a leader you have most likely spent a lot of time wondering about your job and your role. You have thought about expectations you have for yourself, as well as the expectations people around you have about your position. You have probably started, and ended, many days trying to crack the mystery as to why some days feel like things are coming together and you're turning a corner with the team to go to the next level, but then other days feel like you are sliding backwards and things are rapidly unraveling around you. Chances are you have taken inventory of this path you are on as you reflect on how you got here and if you like it here, while other days you are simply plotting your fastest exit strategy out of here. Being in a position to inspire and motivate people, while simultaneously being accountable and responsible for the end result, can be a challenge that has undone even the most dedicated among us. There are so many moving parts to this leadership piece, and people struggle with how to do something that seems to continuously be "in process" and you're never quite done. There isn't a beginning and end to this role, as it is a quintessential journey. A journey filled with breathtaking moments of flawless perfection—which are tragically accompanied by a seemingly endless barrage of frustration (and jaw-dropping surprise at the range & scope of the random situations sitting in your path to be respectfully and competently addressed!). People need a full tool box of skills and strategies to help them show up every day and have the kind of impact they want to have on the people in their lives, because otherwise they stay stuck in the whirl of doing what they have always done—even if it hasn't worked.

The Dream Boss is a direct result of training and coaching countless managers/supervisors, and their teams, around how to effectively build emotional intelligence skills (or people skills). The skills and tools in *The Dream Boss* have an audience beyond those with a boss title on a business card because at some point, in some way, everyone is "in charge" somewhere in their lives.

People are supervising, leading or managing people at work, at home, at school, at church, in the community and within a family. Bottom line is, whoever you are, wherever you are, you have a lot of people in your world—and it takes infinite skills to manage all of those relationships in a positive way. People bring joy, laughter and infinite "wow" moments in to our lives. But those same people also have the capacity to bring challenges, stress, and frustration. Emotional intelligence skills are never about changing/shifting/fixing the other person, because that doesn't work. Building your emotional intelligence is all about helping you successfully handle whatever situation you are in so you can maintain a positive, powerful and professional state.

Although the title is, *The Dream Boss* this book about effective leadership is actually more about how people build relationships in their world and not connected to role or title. This material has been covered in the nonprofit world with senior leaders, direct line staff, and clients those agencies serve. It has been shared with Adult Basic Education providers, administrators/faculty at colleges, and K-12 educators. It has been taught to people working for both small and large businesses, entrepreneurs working at home, as well as people who are currently working as they raise children. *The Dream Boss* is about people and the book provides a range of transferable tools and strategies people can immediately apply and use in whatever circles they are leading. As a trainer and a coach I am grateful for the extensive, ongoing feedback I have received over the years around these tools, including what challenges people as well as what works. My hope is something in here will work for you.

Much success,
Carrie

The real voyage of discovery consists not in seeking new lands but seeing with new eyes.

–Marcel Proust

Introduction

P eople want to be successful when they are the leader. They want to support individuals and teams to reach individual and collective goals. That sounds logical because when someone is in charge it should not come as a surprise to know most people really want to do a good job at it.

Unfortunately here is where things can get tricky. People may know they want it, but they don't know how to go about doing it. People struggle being the kind of leader they would like to be despite putting in a lot of time, energy, and effort.

People have said they feel optimistic about managing the team when they are sitting at home drinking coffee and diligently developing a profoundly proactive plan for the upcoming day. But, when they get to the office it never seems to quite work out the way they planned. Matter of fact, many times it flows more like a bad sitcom and not the Emmy award winning script they had created hours earlier.

The morning fantasy about meeting with the team to plan the next project, with everyone excited and engaged, never quite materializes. The individual supervisions, with employees coming in prepared with thoughtful reflections of their performance and eager to look at how to improve productivity and expand their contribution to the team? Sounded hopeful, but that doesn't happen either. And the appreciations, acknowledgments and affirmations you were hoping would be shared with reckless abandon throughout unit meetings? Nine hours at the office and there wasn't even a flicker of something positive shared by anyone, at any meeting, at any point, during the long and draining day. Nothing even remotely resembles a speck of the morning's delusional wishes, and it's only Monday.

Sound familiar? If you're a manager, leader, or supervisor in any capacity in your world, there's a good chance something about this resonates with you. For many of you it more than resonates. It is clicking in a big, big way.

It's draining and overwhelming to feel like as the leader you need to bring the magic, as well as find the magic in everyone around you, every day. Not just sometimes, but all the time. Every day, every meeting, every conversation. It's a lot, and it's not a surprise this leads to massive burnout and a whole lot of white flags going up from people who just can't do the whole inspiration-and-motivation thing for another second.

It's good to know that you're not alone, but beyond the shallow sense of peace that comes from confirmation you're in good company, you know this just isn't good enough. You know this could be better and you could be better. You are ready to go all in because you cannot continue living this predictable, bland, and uninspired script for the rest of your days. That just cannot be an option.

You want your team to go to the next level, because you are ready to go to the next level, and you are prepared to make this happen by trying some new tools, strategies and perspectives. Some of you may feel like you don't care about being a dream anything—you just want to be just a halfway decent leader that people don't hate, and that is fine too. Wherever you're at, or whatever you aspire to be, if you're looking to grow there are tools in here for you to try.

WHAT GOES IN TO THE MAKING OF A DREAM BOSS?

There are many components to it, but based on conversations with hundreds and hundreds of people it became clear it can be distilled down to three areas, Powerful, Positive, and Professional.

1 POWERFUL: KNOW — They *know* how to succeed, as well as how to support others to succeed

2 POSITIVE: LIKE — They genuinely *like* who they are, what they are doing, and the people/world around them.

3 PROFESSIONAL: MODEL — They consistently *model*, by what they say and what they do: boundaries, respect, and integrity.

The three components of *The Dream Boss* foundation certainly applies to leaders, but they also encompass key people skills all people benefit from having, and they include:

1 POWERFUL: KNOW

Powerful: having great power, prestige, or influence—a leader

The Dream Boss is Powerful. This power establishes your credibility. *The Dream Boss* is comfortable owning the power that comes with the role of being in charge. This is not about being on a power trip, or dangling power over the team, which some mistakenly attribute to establishing power. True power does not need to be stated.

Power is something one feels, and comes from confidence, clarity, and vision. You trust you have what it takes to be a leader and people around you believe you can lead them. If they didn't feel you were solid in your power they would wonder, "How can I follow you, if I don't know/trust that you know how to lead me?" It is imperative you believe you have the ability to lead, because if you don't believe it how would you ever convince anyone else you are qualified to be in charge?

Being Powerful is the foundation of being *The Dream Boss*.

Here are some examples of what being **POWERFUL** looks like:

- Clear on the bigger picture (mission/vision/future)
- Experienced
- Insight
- Has a plan on how to achieve bigger picture
- Solid
- Understands the impact of power and what it means to be a leader
- Shares power & knows sharing it doesn't diminish it
- Confident
- Leader
- Strong sense of ownership, responsibility, and accountability for self and others
- Ability to adeptly celebrate/acknowledge successes, as well as support team through challenges/struggles
- Steady in a crisis
- Competent, knowledgeable

What does being **POWERFUL** mean to you?

- In your life, where do you feel like you are *Powerful?*
- As a leader, where do you feel like you are *Powerful?*
- Where would you like to expand/grow/develop in this area?

 POSITIVE: **LIKE**

Positive: having a good effect: favorable—a role model marked by optimism

The Dream Boss is Positive. There is an energy that comes from the positive that draws people in, builds relationships, and cultivates investment. Being positive is appealing and focusing on the positive is an energy boost. People want to be around positive people and this pull has a tremendous effect on the culture and climate when that positive person is the boss.

Some of you may feel resistant or even a little cynical around a focus on the positive because of past experiences with people deemed to be "too nice" or those you believed were taken advantage of because of their good nature. Before going any further it's important to clarify a few things. Being positive is not about smiling while ignoring or hiding from issues. It is not about being a Pollyanna who believes all is well, all the time, with everyone. It should never be confused with weakness, passivity, naiveté, or a displaced desire to be liked by everyone, at any cost. Certainly not every day is about smiles, hugs, sunshine and high fives. There are many days, or weeks, or painfully long stretches of time that feel like they hold none of those things, yet it is still possible for a leader to be fundamentally positive.

Being a positive leader is about looking for what is right, what is working, what is getting done, what is going well, and what is succeeding. It means being a leader looking to build upon the strengths of individuals, teams, and systems in a way that encourages growth and movement.

Being positive means the spotlight is on supporting success, while challenges and obstacles are approached with the intention of addressing them, and then getting right back on board with moving forward and reaching goals.

Being positive is a foundational framework that shapes how a person moves through the world, impacting how someone both interprets and experiences daily life. A positive lens not only serves to enhance one's life, but has the capacity to positively touch the lives of all of those around them. Quite simply, when people are grounded in the positive they seek it out and celebrate it wherever they are, including at work. When leaders are positive it has an impact on the team and level of connection and investment people have in their work.

Here are some examples of what being **POSITIVE** looks like:

- Optimistic
- Looks for what is right, working, getting done, going well
- Believes in people
- Enjoys the work
- Strength-based approach
- Accessible and approachable (smiles, laughs, outgoing)
- Sense of trust (self and others)
- Forward moving, future focused
- Steady, calm, even keeled, on daily basis as well as in crisis
- Solid perspective
- Realistic
- Generous with appreciation, gratitude and thanks
- Supports learning, especially during challenges/obstacles/ failures
- Celebrates successes, acknowledges contributions

What does being **POSITIVE** mean to you?

- In your life, where do you feel like you are *Positive*?
- As a leader, where do you feel like you are *Positive*?
- Where would you like to expand/grow/develop in this area?

❸ PROFESSIONAL: **MODEL**

Professional: exhibiting a courteous, conscientious, and generally businesslike manner in the workplace

The Dream Boss is Professional. Many leaders will say, "Of course I'm professional, since you must be professional if you're in charge!" Interesting assumption, but not necessarily true.

It's important to remember being professional is not determined by what you wear, where your office is, or what title/position is on your business card. It is not about your degree, or the length of time you have been in the job. It's not about how many people you manage, or how many meetings you run. It is not about the things people typically rattle off to prove they are professional.

Being professional is more complicated than people realize. It is about how you navigate the world of emotions, your own as well as people on your team, which surface while on the job, and while moving through daily life. Being professional is about how you treat all employees, even the ones you may not like. Being professional is about how you communicate, model behaviors, maintain boundaries, and create a climate and culture of equality that fosters growth and productivity. A great way to remember the range and scope of what it means to be Professional is to imagine you are being held up as the example of "how to" handle something, approach something, respond to someone, etc. You are the example of what it looks like when it is done right, or well, or at the highest level. This approach can often help leaders reflect on their actions and interactions in a more thoughtful and self-reflective way.

A lot of people assume they must have somehow mastered the skill of being professional, just by nature of climbing the career ladder and becoming the boss. Unfortunately you don't have to look very hard to see that's not how it works, as being professional does not innately accompany any role or job description. This has proved to be the area where there is the largest gap between where people perceive themselves to be in contrast to how others see them. People will admit to feeling like they could do more to be Powerful and work on how they show up to lead, and people will openly talk about how much they could grow in being more Positive as a leader. But, when it comes to Professional, people will say they have this one down and they are convinced they do it well. It is imperative leaders are open to exploring this area in an honest and real way, because this can be a significant gap for many leaders and holds people back in their success with leadership. The good news is, with the right approach this one can be a quick fix!

Here are examples of what **PROFESSIONAL** looks like:

Clear boundaries

High standards/expectations

Consistent

Sense of equality (no "double standards" or hypocrisy)

Fair

Attention to detail

Ethical

Models Ownership, Responsibility, Accountability

Expertly handle emotions (self and others)

Strong communicator

Investment in growth/learning/education

Transparent (no hidden agendas)

What does being **PROFESSIONAL** mean to you?

In your life, where do you feel like you are *Professional*?

As a leader, where do you feel like you are *Professional*?

Where would you like to expand/grow/develop in this area?

*When we seek to discover
the best in others,
we somehow bring out
the best in ourselves.*

–William Arthur Ward

CHAPTER ————

1

Purpose of the Dream Boss

A s you read this book, do a little research of your own and try asking people, "Have you ever had a terrible boss? A boss who was a real nightmare to work for and you couldn't get out fast enough?" You will probably find most people reply, "Yes! I certainly have!" Then you will hear story after story about what the boss (es) did, or did not do, to secure a top notch spot on the, "Worst Boss Ever" list. You may even have that list too. It could be going back to your first job, 15 years old and selling pizza, but you remember all the gory details of working for someone who embodied what doesn't work when you're the boss. If you are fortunate enough to not have any direct experience in this area, you have certainly endured endless tales of bad boss woes from all of your nearest and dearest.

After establishing what doesn't work in a boss, notice what happens when you ask people, "Have you ever had an amazing boss? A boss that you will forever remember and appreciate for what they did and how they did it?" As you listen notice the smiles, the faraway look in the eyes, and the nostalgic tone in the voice (or, if it's a current boss, the way the voice goes up a few octaves with excitement, glee and maybe even a little flaunting!). People typically don't have as many examples of the boss(es) that rocked their worlds, because that is a special category reserved for only the best, but it is clear they cherish the ones they have. Perhaps you aren't even here right now because you have a faraway twinkle in your eye, remembering the time you worked for someone who firmly secured a spot at the top of your "Best Of" list!

What is up with this managing/supervising thing? Why does it seem to happen so easily for some while others really struggle with it? It's a fascinating conundrum because people skills are the foundation to successfully managing and supervising, yet we don't seem to teach, or even talk about, people skills. We just hope people with a title will somehow innately know what to do and connect the dots in a profound and powerful way as they lead teams to greatness. At this point it's becoming clear all the hoping isn't translating to much—and we might need to do more than just hope. It could be time to start doing things differently.

Where should we start doing things differently? We could start with preparation, training, and support. If there isn't a lot of training or preparation on how to lead, then how do people typically become the leader? For a lot of people it looks something like this, "Great news! If you show up, do a good job, and give everything you have, you will be promoted! You will run this department (team, program, unit). Play your cards right and you'll become the boss of the people that used to be your peers!"

The rest of that statement should be, "But, we regret to inform you we won't be able to help you develop your management, leadership, or supervision skills, and we don't really have any thoughts on how to do it, or how to do it better. Please just try really hard every day and do the best you can!" Or maybe it's more like this, "Congratulations! You are brilliant and you know your content, so you're hired and you'll be the boss now! See you Monday when you meet your big team and take over this troubled department!"

This person has the education and experience for the content part of the work, but content is only half of the equation. What about the process piece? That is where the team needs a leader's skill, and that crucial piece is often missing.

Working with hundreds of managers/supervisors and teams around how to develop emotional intelligence skills (also known as people skills or soft skills), I have been asked over and over, "What are the key things managers, leaders and supervisors need to know?" I looked at my work over the years and targeted the pieces that kept consistently emerging as the most common areas people struggle with when working with people. Those pieces, and the models created to help people get traction in those areas, became the foundation for *The Dream Boss*.

This book isn't just for leaders/managers, as it is filled with tips that could be relevant for all people. These are tools everyone could add to their tool box with the potential to improve their lives personally and professionally. Whoever you are, you are managing/leading or supervising on some level, somewhere in your life. Maybe it is a department at work, or the parents at your child's school. Maybe you run a multi-million dollar department, or perhaps you supervise a team at an after-school program, or you are a work-from-home entrepreneur. You could have two part-time people you manage, or a volunteer group of 800 that you want to take to the next level. The skills in this book are relevant for people who cross paths with other people, so if you have people in your life, there is something in here for you.

This book is the result of people over the years saying that they wanted a guide book, or play book, or cheat sheet on how to be better with people. Based on all the trainings, coaching and supervisions I have done with people, as well as extensive conversations I have had with both managers/supervisors and their teams, here it is. The purpose of sharing this information is because these tools consistently appear to have interest and value for people, and perhaps most importantly, they have worked.

*If I have the belief that
I can do it, I shall surely
acquire the capacity to do
it even if I may not have
it at the beginning.*

–Mahatma Gandhi

2

The "It Factor"

Have you ever met someone and you immediately really liked this person? And you weren't alone in this—because it seemed like everybody else seemed to really like this person too. This appeal, or draw, that some people have isn't a mystery or some kind of unknown phenomenon—there is a name for it. It's what called the "It Factor". People who have "It" are the people others respond positively to—and want to be around. These "It Factor" people are people many of us want to be, people we want to have in our lives, and people we all want to work for. If these people are so appealing and we want to be around them and work for them, what is it that they actually do, or don't do, that puts them in this category?

The "It Factor" isn't as elusive as many think. We have already established the actions and behaviors of the most enigmatic leaders all fall within the Powerful, Positive, and Professional categories. If it's already defined, why doesn't everyone just follow that roadmap to leadership mastery? Simple. People do the best they can, with what they have, and most people don't have the skills/tools they need to do things differently (or better). This is what has to change. We need to talk more about these soft skills, or people skills, people need to be able to build successful relationships.

The majority of our lives are spent in the workplace and we all deserve, including managers/supervisors, to have a successful and positive experience at work. I've never met a supervisor who wakes up and decides that today s/he will thoughtfully and intentionally moves in to the day with the goal of wreaking havoc on staff. Nobody heads in to the office thinking, "I'd really like to make the life of every member of my team a living hell today. My goal is to see how many people will think about quitting. I will be really successful if over 80% of the team actually logs on to a job search site today at lunch!"

No, that is never the case and it may surprise you to discover many managers and supervisors are filled with daily stress and anxiety over how to do a better job. Even the boss winning top billing in your "Worst Ever" category was actually trying to do a good job. It may be hard for you to believe, but even those bosses wanted to be successful at positively leading the team. What is the problem then? Everyone is doing the best they can with what they have but sometimes people simply don't have the right tools.

What are the "right tools?" And what is it that the successful managers are doing? I have had the remarkable experience of asking hundreds and hundreds of people the same two questions and regardless of the group demographics I have received similar answers. I've asked people 18 years old, working after school for three years, and people 68 years old working, as one woman proudly proclaimed, "for two of your lifetimes!" The experiences and insights people have shared are consistent across age, ethnicity, gender, income, education, title, or position.

Before you see what people shared, first see what you think in the activity below because if you participate as we go it will be the easiest way to ensure you're connecting to the tools/strategies in the book.

Activity: The "It Factor" — PART 1
Define What Does NOT Work

Have you ever had a terrible supervisor?

- A supervisor who can barely inspire you to blink and breathe, never mind go to the next level professionally?

- A supervisor you will forever remember because he/she was the living embodiment of what does **not** work?

- A supervisor who asked you to come in on a Saturday and your first thought was, "Are you kidding? Not unless this is explicitly stated on my job description!"

No actual names are needed here, but what did this boss do or not do, to make them so memorable in this way? Can you define it?

Take a minute and write down the traits that come to mind.

(*You actually need to do this, because activities in the book only work if you do them!)

What does *NOT* work:

Group identified examples of what does **NOT** work

Based on hundreds and hundreds of replies, from people 18 years old to 82 years old, it's fascinating how similar the lists always are. Every list has some combination/variation of the traits and skills below:

- Hypocritical/double standards
- Entitled/inflated self-importance
- Has favorites, and/or targets
- Doesn't listen
- Never says "thank you"
- Moody/angry/snaps/yells
- Doesn't do what they say they will, lies
- Negative
- Takes all the credit/shifts all blame or responsibility
- Promises things they don't or won't do/no follow through
- Ineffective communicator
- Unprofessional
- Poor boundaries
- Doesn't seek input or feedback
- Condescending
- Believes they are better/more important
- No structure
- Hostile/cold/distant/detached
- Dismissive
- Micromanaging
- Tells, never asks
- Egocentric/narcissistic
- Unpredictable/inconsistent
- Not mission focused/lack of vision or bigger picture
- Explosive/tantrums
- Overwhelmed/can't perform job requirements

After naming what doesn't work, now we want to name what *does* work. We will now define the illustrious "It Factor".

Have you ever had a supervisor that was magic and you knew you were in the midst of something amazing? It was as if you hit the lottery and you knew it. Matter of fact, the whole team felt lucky and people actually enjoyed the work and working together! When you talked about your work you knew others envied you and you knew this manager would make the short list of "WOW" bosses that you would have in your lifetime. You thought this person was amazing at his/her job, and the way they did *their* job, made you love *your* job. If you were asked to come in on a Saturday, you'd say, "Absolutely...and I'll stop and pick up the bagels/coffee on my way in!" They embodied the "It Factor" and became the benchmark for what *The Dream Boss* means to you.

What was "it?" What did they do that made them memorable? Right now, take a minute to define the traits, skills, strengths, attributes and actions of your "WOW" boss.

For the few of you out there that have NOT had a magical boss, think about bosses that friends/family have had that fall in to this category. Even if you haven't directly experienced it, you know people that have— because they told you all about their "amazing" boss, all the time, so use their experiences to help you do this next activity. How do I know they incessantly talked about their amazing boss? Because people always do.

The "It Factor": What Works

Group identified examples of the "It Factor":

Based on the list below, the boss that stands out and held in high regard by so many clearly embodies what it means to be positive, powerful and professional.

- Respect
- Approachable/available
- Appreciative/Says "thank you"
- Constructive feedback
- Positive attitude
- Collaborates
- Listens
- Cares/invested
- Boundaries
- Trust/hands off
- Empathetic
- Passion for work
- Professionalism
- Laughs/happy/sense of fun
- Energetic
- Willing to work with team
- Follows same standards, norms and expectations as team
- Equal treatment of all staff
- Inspires/motivates people
- Organized
- Solid/stable/consistent
- Ability to apologize/admit mistakes/learns from challenges
- Mentor
- Willing to do what needs to be done/jumps in/pitches in
- Vision
- Commitment to professional development and growth
- Accessible
- Integrity/word is "good"

Why do this activity?

The purpose is to help people understand from their own experiences they already know what works, and what doesn't work. Establishing these "norms" about what makes an effective supervisor from personal experience enables people to look at things through a different lens. It helps people to reflect on their actions/behaviors, as well as opens the door to recognize individual strengths and areas for growth. Self-reflection is the only way to figure out what you already know, and where you may want to grow.

It's important to acknowledge we most likely will find ourselves on both lists, as we all have areas of success/mastery and we are all capable of demonstrating less than desirable management/leadership skills. And yes, "all of us" actually includes you, too.

The question becomes, if we are on both lists, what do we do?

How do we make sure that we're developing and building more of the "It Factor" skills of *The Dream Boss*, and not staying stuck in the, "what doesn't work" category?

Are people who have the "It Factor" perfect? No, they are actually far from it. Sometimes they messed up, some days they dropped the ball. They have been wrong, or snappy, or limited in their vision, or their skills. They may forget things, sometimes they have bad ideas, and they have been known to make a bad call. They still have "It" but it's not because they are perfect.

They embody the "It Factor" because even when they were imperfect, they handled it with finesse. If they messed up, they owned it. If they dropped the ball, they named it. If they were wrong or snappy, they apologized and didn't attempt to minimize or deflect what they did. They successfully handle and manage their emotions, and if/when they didn't, they were quick to recognize it and respond appropriately to own, address and apologize for their actions. The "It Factor" isn't about only having powerful, positive, professional, or perfect emotions; it's about *handling* your emotions powerfully, positively, professionally. Being human means we are imperfect, but developing key emotional intelligence skills means you're able to navigate the messy and hard parts that comes from interacting with other people.

We all have an innate understanding of what the magic is, which is fabulous. It's great to name who the great ones are, but isn't it even better to be one? Do you want to be a leader who embodies the "It Factor"? Of course you do, so let's figure out how to do that.

> *If you want to be successful, know what you are doing, love what you are doing, and believe in what you are doing.*
>
> –Will Rogers

3

DCI Model©

The Say Yes Institute builds all coaching, training and workshops around the **D**efine, **C**larify and **I**mplement (DCI) Model©. This three part model was created as a concrete tool to support a thoughtful assessment of personal/professional goals, determine why those goals are important, and develop a specific plan of action to reach those goals. The DCI Model© works because it is direct and clearly focused on developing a comprehensive strategy to reach/achieve each identified goal.

Participants are encouraged to explore the DCI Model© through a series of thought provoking questions and interactive/reflective activities. This has been proven to be an effective strategy, both with individuals and within groups, because it quickly fosters a sense of focus and inspires direct action.

The DCI Model© supports participants to formulate clear goals, as well as own clarity around their investment in reaching those goals. The steps then help participants to develop a comprehensive and achievable plan of implementation with clear goals, timelines, plans of accountability and tools to assess progress and validate successes. Every skill/ strategy in this book will be explored through the DCI Model© in order to help give it context and provide you with a blueprint to achieve personal and professional success.

DCI MODEL©: *How to reach a goal*

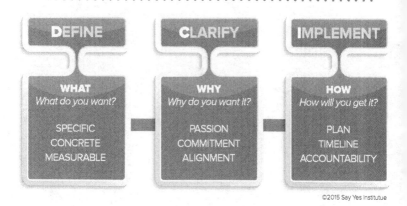

DEFINE	CLARIFY	IMPLEMENT
WHAT	**WHY**	**HOW**
What do you want?	*Why do you want it?*	*How will you get it?*
SPECIFIC	PASSION	PLAN
CONCRETE	COMMITMENT	TIMELINE
MEASURABLE	ALIGNMENT	ACCOUNTABILITY

©2015 Say Yes Institutue

The three steps of the DCI Model© are:

Define: WHAT

This step supports exploration around the many layers of defining the "what" part of your goals. You need to know, specifically and concretely, exactly what you want to achieve. This covers the specific questions of "how much, how many, by when?" Your goal needs to be measurable, otherwise how will you know when you reach it? Many people set generic and ambiguous goals which cannot be measured, such as "be more successful." Vague goal setting translates to a vague victory. How will you know when it's time to celebrate your success if you have never clearly named what it would look like? Make sure your goal is framed in the positive, and is specific enough that you will know when you have achieved it.

> ## Use these questions to help you define the "**WHAT**" of the goal you want to reach:
>
> - What is your specific, concrete and measurable goal? (How much, how many, by when?)
> - What would having it mean for you, or do for you?
> - What is of value to you about that goal?
> - What does your goal look like when you've reached it, or how will you know you have reached it?

Clarify: WHY

This step illuminates the "why" part of the process and generates clarity around why a goal is worth achieving and warrants your valuable time and attention. Many goals are defined on the intellectual level however a mental belief that it is a good/positive/logical goal isn't going to be enough to get you there if a person has no clear connection to the goal. If something isn't alignment with the goal, or the heart isn't in it, the person isn't going to do it.

The "why" will drive you forward when there are challenges/obstacles or barriers. When a person succeeds at a goal it is often because having an authentic alignment supports focus and determination, even where there are bumps in the road. This step reminds us we invest in what we believe in and are committed to, not just what may appear logical or sound. It is the heart part of the goal that builds commitment which ensures the follow through needed to make things happen.

Investment comes from connecting with the heart part of the goal, but once you have that clarity you become unstoppable. Clarity builds commitment and ultimately ensures you have the follow through needed to makes things happen—and push through challenges.

Use these questions to help you clarify the **"WHY"** of the goal you want to reach:

- Why are you invested in reaching your goal?
- Why do you feel a sense of passion, commitment or alignment around this goal?
- Why is this goal a priority for you?
- Why would reaching this goal be of value to you, your work, and your life?

Implement: HOW

The final step focused on the concrete "how" around implementation plans and details specific actions needed to achieve your goal. A clear implementation plan is foundational to your success. You need to know what actions you will take, how you will take them, and how you will move through roadblocks and challenges.

Well formed goals, even with a high level of passion and alignment, can still idle indefinitely if there is no plan for action. It is also important to decide how, if at all, you will be accountable for reaching your goal. Some people do best with external accountability and need to build in some way to have follow-up with others, while others excel with only internal accountability. It's important to clearly name all of the components that encompass the "how" of your implementation phase.

Use these questions to help you determine a solid action/implementation plan around **HOW** you will reach your goal:

How will you develop a plan and timeline for reaching this goal?

How will you know you have achieved your goal?

How will you address any barriers, challenges or obstacles?

How/to whom will you be accountable?

To support maximum growth and application of new skills and tools, all activities in the book will be presented and processed through the DCI Model©. It's not enough for people to read an activity and think, "Wow, that's interesting." Thinking something is interesting isn't enough of a catalyst to trigger action and application. Simply noting something seems logical or could be useful doesn't transfer to actually doing something. The goal is to have people read about an activity, try on a new perspective, and then have an immediate and executable plan for application.

To take it one step further, and in the interest of full transparency, the hope is you will read it, "get" it, and then head in to your world to use it! Clarity doesn't come from sitting on the couch, so the only way for you to acquire new skills and tools is for you to actually do something new. The DCI Model© will help make sure you're ready for action as you integrate these new skills and tools in to your life.

Our chief want is someone who will inspire us to be what we know we could be.

–Ralph Waldo Emerson

CHAPTER

4

Powerful: KNOW

Y ou're a leader and you're in charge. Because of your role, you have power. This means whether you agree or not, and whether you like it or not, you are powerful.

It's interesting how many people in positions of power have never thought about what the word means. They have never connected the dots around what it means to have power, or how to best use that power to positively impact their world or the people in it.

Why does that happen and how are people in positions of power so often oblivious to the kind of impact their role has on others? Through information gathered from training and coaching it seems to come down to two reasons. The first reason is typically because the person was promoted without ever receiving training on what kinds of skills are needed to successfully lead a group/team. The second reason is often because a person is incredibly knowledgeable and talented around content, or the "what" part of the job, but never received training on the process, or the "how."

Did you read that and think, "*Wait, aren't both of those reasons about lack of training?*" You are correct. There is actually one reason why people have a tough time with managing/leading others, and it comes down to lack of training. People can't give what they don't have, and they can't do what they don't know. Without the training, support, and skills/tools necessary to lead effectively, people will struggle with it. There is no mystery to what is going awry here. Leaders know it, and their teams know it, so in the best interest of all parties to address this gap.

What are the kinds of things that people in leadership roles are saying?

Here are a few thoughts from some managers/supervisors. Can you relate to any of these, or does any of this sound or feel familiar to you?

Activity: What Went Wrong?

If you heard someone saying the things below, what would you be thinking? If you had to determine what may have gone awry with their leadership, what would you come up with?

"I guess it (the reorganization) could be taken the wrong way, since the team didn't know the whole story. It made sense to me, but I can see how it wouldn't make sense to them, which is why we're dealing with this big crisis of trust now." –Director

"I feel like everything I do is wrong. It's like I can't get them (team) to take initiative and everything feels like a struggle." –Executive Director

"I just lay it on the line. I keep telling them what's not working, because I'm hoping they will do something differently, but nothing is changing. It's actually getting worse." –Team Supervisor

"We are probably in this position because I didn't handle things in the way I should have when they initially happened. I thought things would work themselves out, but they never did and I let it go for too long." –Manager

"To be honest I just keep hoping that some people will give their notice, because I need people in here that are willing to work, and that I can work with. I know some people are dealing with a lot in their lives, but I can't keep doing their jobs. It's just too much." –Team Leader

Process: What Went Wrong?

In the space below, you are the coach/consultant coming in to help respond to these issues. Write down what you think might be happening with the managers/directors/leaders.

- What do you think they may be doing, or not doing, to contribute to the issues they are dealing with at work?

- What could be present, or absent, in the culture/climate?

- Where do you think leadership needs to direct attention in order to effectively address these issues?

Thoughts:

Process:

**What did you come up with? You probably identified
some of the following areas:**

Lack of communication

Issues with ownership

Being negative/punitive

Not dealing with issues, denial, avoidance

Lack of vision

No relationships/connection to staff

Double standards/possible inconsistencies

Lack of clarity around how to support/lead/direct the team

Owning too much/taking on too much/doing too much

It can be easy to determine what is missing when you're looking at someone else's performance, or reflecting on the struggles/challenges with someone else's team, but it is harder to see when it's you or your team. How do things go so wrong for so many managers and supervisors? And, more importantly, how can people make things better?

In all of the conversations with people around the key qualities of the most effective leaders there were several which kept coming up, but one stood out. The most powerful leaders had a clear, strong, consistent commitment to equality. A foundation of equality lends itself to trust, and a leader holding the trust of a group has a great deal of power.

What does equality mean? It means things are unequivocally equal, with all people, all the time. That is an incredibly challenging state to maintain, especially because the reality is you actually don't like everyone the same. You don't find everyone equally appealing, you don't view everyone on your team in an equally favorable light, and you certainly don't think everyone on your team performs equally. You may know it, and I certainly know it, but your team will never know it.

Members of your team will never be privy to the possibility you find some people a dash more spectacular than others. To take it one step further, if it were ever revealed you had favorites, people would be beyond shocked. The group would be floored to hear that you can't stand Myrtle or Howard and you wouldn't care if they searched for a new job on company time. Nobody would ever know your true feelings—not from meetings or supervisions and not from any of your conversations or actions, because you handle your emotions. You are tapped in to the importance of treating everyone equally, in all ways, at all times. That ability is the sign of a mature boss and takes tremendous skill, awareness, and practice.

It takes skill to remember you are always on. When you're tired, when your car breaks down, when you're dealing with a family drama, you are still on. When you have a headache, when you're annoyed with your brother, when you find out your accountant made a significant error in your taxes, you are still on. You always remember you are a leader and people are watching everything you say, and everything you do, all the time. This has endless ramifications for you and all of your actions or reactions. Fair or unfair, you are always in a position to be held up as an example or model on how to handle yourself appropriately and act in a consistent and predictable way. The example you set is inextricably linked to how powerful you are in the eyes of your team—and your ability to adhere to principals of equality, even when tired, or stressed, or annoyed, should be impressively consistent!

Beyond a commitment to equality, how can you build up your skills to own the role of being Powerful? How can you make sure you are saying and doing things that contribute to your efforts to become *The Dream Boss?* Here are four tools/strategies to help you become a more Powerful leader:

 Leadership CHOICE:
Power of Your Daily Decisions

"The better my mood is, the better the team seems to be. I used to think that my mood was a result of the day, but now I see that my mood actually sets the stage for the day. When I'm positive, everything is better and I really want to have more of those days!" –Assistant Director

What if the catalyst for the quality and content of your day wasn't about the luck of the draw, or the stars aligning? What if it wasn't about having perfect weather, or the right outfit, or your favorite sandwich for lunch? What if there was no big mystery as to why some days are simply amazing, while others feel like an endless barrage of unbearable misery? What if the determining factor wasn't a hidden mystery and it was simply about you?

The great news is, it is about you. You are the one with the power to determine how your day unfolds. You may not be aware of this, but every single day you make choices which determine how you interpret your day. You choose how you are going to experience every conversation, exchange, and event in your world. This isn't a secret inside scoop that only some people are told, while the rest are left in the dark. The fact is, every day you are in control of what you choose to focus on, and how you choose to direct your energy.

Another way to think about this is this: Every day you take countless positions on people, events, experiences etc., and then you set out to prove your position is correct by the proof/evidence you gather during the day. If you think it's going to be a great day, the team is going to do great things, and you are going to love your job, then you will be able to prove that at the end of the day because you will have a lot of examples supporting that position. If you think it's going to be a horrible day, the team is dysfunctional and lazy, you hate your job, you are underappreciated and the world is a miserable place, at the end of the day you could prove that, too. You are amazing at proving your position, whatever position you take. Unfortunately most people aren't aware of what position they are busy proving, and many are shocked to find they have been busy taking chronically negative and deficit-based positions on everyone and everything in their lives.

People get a little cranky when they hear this. People are invested in believing life happens *to* them, not *from* them. People talk about their moods/attitudes as if they have no control over them, or that those moods/attitudes are inflicted upon them by outside sources. It is important to remember that nothing, no experience or action or event, has any inherent meaning, good or bad. This means we the ones assigning meaning, and the moments of our lives are nothing more, or less, than the meaning we give them.

Do you see where this is going? You control your focus and your energy. It is an ongoing choice, and the choice is yours. Every day your world and the people in it, including the people at work, are viewed based on how you choose to direct your energy and your focus. You take positions on people, then you give their words/actions meaning based on how you decide to direct your focus and energy.

Your daily choices really matter. Not understanding the importance or the implications of those choices has caused some grief for many, many bosses. When you choose to channel your focus or your energy on the negative, it can create a mess—and a short memory on your end does not equal a short memory on their end. You had a bad firing back in 1988? There's still talk of that. Your little situation (or we could call it a tantrum or quasi-explosion) at a meeting three years ago? There's still residue from that around the office. That employee you gave a warning to for doing something you had done the week before? You may have forgotten about it, but they still can't get over that one. You can say this isn't fair, it's ridiculous to even talk about those things because it's over, and that was an anomaly because it's not how you usually are, but guess what? As the boss, and because of your power, that's just not how it works. Your choices matter.

Whenever working with teams around issues of conflict, trust, low morale, or performance issues, it will often connect back to something that happened in the past that leadership may not have dealt with right, or fully, or openly, or honestly, or to completion. Why does this happen? We need to remember leaders are powerful, and whatever is said or done, as well as what is not said or not done, sends a message.

This means when you're stressed, when you're cranky, when you're tired, when you're just "off," you are still sending a message. As the leader you are still holding the identity of being powerful, whether you're in the midst of an incredibly amazing day, or a remarkably bad and uninspired day. If things are not handled well by the leader it will resurface indefinitely and cause ongoing issues in the culture/climate of an organization or group. The decisions you make matter.

The Leadership CHOICE model can help provide a visual to how the element of choice plays out in your world every day.

Leadership CHOICE illustrates how the focus/energy of a leader can impact a team, leading to very different results. When leaders choose to direct their focus/energy to the positive, it has an impact on people. This impact contributes to overwhelming positive results in terms of what happens for/with the team. If leaders choose to direct their focus/energy towards the negative this also has a significant impact on the group, however with negative results. It is important to remind people this is always a choice. Every time you act, interact, or react, you are making a choice. Again, some people tell me they aren't "choosing" anything—they

The Leadership CHOICE Model

©2015 Say Yes Institutue

are just responding to what is happening. That reply never holds because as a leader how you choose to act and react is always a choice. It is important to stay connected to the power you have as a leader and be diligent with how you choose how you direct your focus and energy.

This model serves as a reminder for people in leadership positions about the power of their focus and energy. The positive is an energy boost, and the negative is an energy drain. Every time you open your mouth or head in to an interaction you impact people, and that impact has a direct result. You are always in a role with the power to move the group in one direction or the other. Most people will acknowledge the importance of moving the group in a positive direction because they know it will get more done and generate more productive results. But this positive focus doesn't just happen, and it's certainly not something some people innately have the ability or gift to do, while others do not, because nobody is born with the "choose the positive" gene. This is a choice people have countless opportunities to make every day—and the more people in leadership roles pay attention to it, the greater the impact and results are for everyone.

Action: Leadership CHOICE

Explore the Leadership CHOICE you are making on a daily basis. Where do you think you are directing your focus and your energy? How does this impact staff? What is the result?

Define: What

What Leadership CHOICE will you commit to making on a daily basis? What situations, circumstances, settings, or people will you focus on? What will you direct your energy toward?

- What is your specific, concrete and measurable goal? (How much, how many, by when?)
- What would having this mean for you, or do for you?
- What is of value to you about that goal?
- What does your goal look like when you've reached it, or how will you know you have reached it?

Clarify: Why

Why is it important to you to make this Leadership CHOICE? Why is this something you are willing to do?

- Why are you invested in reaching your goal?
- Why do you feel a sense of passion, commitment or alignment around this goal?
- Why is this goal a priority for you?
- Why would reaching this goal be of value to you, your work, or your life?

Implement: How

How will you succeed with your new Leadership CHOICE? How will you develop a plan to make this happen?

- How will you develop a plan and timeline for reaching this goal?
- How will you know you have achieved your goal?
- How will you address any barriers, challenges or obstacles?
- How/to whom will you be accountable?

② Castle of Consistency: Power of a Strong and Stable Environment

"If I had to be honest, I know that the rules probably aren't the same for every-one on my team and, at the end of the day, I know that's on me." –Director

This may sound random, but how would you describe a castle? What words immediately come to mind? Would you say it is a fluid structure, continuously in flux, and every day it is a surprise to wake up and see if it is still standing? No, not likely—unless you are describing a sand castle!

You would probably be more inclined to say a castle is a formidable structure, embodying stability. People trust it is consistent, predictable, solid, and strong. Imagine how unsettling it would be for people in the kingdom where the castle was located if every day they awoke to unex-pected (significant or minor) changes in the castle. What feelings would that evoke? What impact would that have? Would the element of the unexpected/unpredictable chip away at their feelings of stability? Would it make people question the leadership, or contribute to people having fears, insecurities, and an overall lack of trust? Would it inevitably cause people to question the viability of the kingdom?

Chances are the ongoing unpredictability would wreak havoc, on every level, with the entire community.

Castles are meant to be solid, predictable and capable of withstanding the test of time. This is important because people do best when they have a literal or figurative structure they can rely on, trust, and expect. This does not mean change and growth cannot happen, it simply means when it does happen it is part of a thoughtful and intentional process, with communication and involvement of all impacted parties.

Now think about your workplace, and the environment you have created for your team, through this lens. Have you built a Castle of Consistency around norms/expectations and overall structure? Are things clear, defined and consistent? Can people trust that there is a process, an order and reliability to the content and the process of their work? Are your procedures, protocols, structures, infrastructure and overall norms something people know, understand and can rely on? Does the team have faith there is a place and a purpose for them?

This model is focused on building stable norms/expectations within a team. It's about building a climate/culture based on fairness, equality and trust that people can consistently predict and expect. It is about ensuring that you have created something solid and stable, embodying power and trust.

Would you say your team culture/climate is solid, like a castle? Or does your culture/climate reflect of the stress/anxiety that accompanies pervasive unpredictability? How do you think you are doing with your ability to maintain consistency with the people you work with?

Activity: Reflection
Do you ever say...

☐ "Well, I don't usually do that, but..."

☐ "I know this isn't how we typically do things, but..."

☐ "No, I would never do that, unless..."

☐ "I wouldn't normally say that, but..."

☐ "I know I did that (said that, emailed that). I typically wouldn't do that, except..."

☐ "I know how it looks (or sounds), but..."

☐ "That's rarely done, but in this particular case..."

Have you ever felt compelled to justify any of your actions with the replies above? You may have done it or said it "but...." as if the "but" would rationalize or validate why you changed the rules, or bent the rules, or did something outside of the established norms. You may want explore your ability to develop consistency if, when asked to explain some of your past actions, behaviors or decisions, your replies include any combination of the replies above.

If you found you are guilty of saying any of those examples, know you are not alone. Those sentences have been used over and over, as people tried to explain why they did or didn't do something, and why the team shouldn't think it would ever happen again. It's important to note the "but..." never qualifies fixes or eliminates anything. Remember how the book started? We talked about how people are watching everything you say and everything you do, all the time, which means even your best "but..." won't ever make it ok.

What does this mean?

As a leader you must reject hypocrisy and all it stands for. If everything you say and do sends a message, you know if it doesn't work for them, it can't work for you. You live by and adhere to same expectations and standards that the team does. If your kid has a little league game, that's important and it's great for you to go to it. Guess what? They have kids too and they'd love to "scoot out early" to catch the game. Or, maybe they don't have kids, but they have family and friends and things that mean a lot to them too. If your schedule is flexible, in order to take in to account your busy and important life, then theirs needs to be too.

If you want your team to be *on* your team, pay close attention to the following as you build a climate and culture of consistency:

- If it applies, or does not apply, to you then it applies, or does not apply, to everyone.

- If there is an established policy/procedure/expectation then it applies to all staff consistently, not just the ones you don't particularly like, or based on your mood that day.

- Be hypersensitive to equality and how that plays out on your team. Know the strongest teams are led by leaders who show up for all of it. It goes a long way for the team to see you pitching in, helping out and participating.

- If you are in charge, you have power. Power means people watch you. People are acutely aware of your actions and highly sensitive to what you say/do with everyone, not just them. People will take notice, and people keep track.

- Keep in mind when people are busy taking stock of not only where they stand with you, but also where others are at with you. This score keeping creates feelings of competition, frustration, drama, discord, discontent, pressure, anxiety and agitation for your team, and for you. If these issues impact your team it is important to look for the gaps/holes and cracks in leadership.

Ultimately, any form of a double standard eats away at the foundational spirit of the team and takes away from your credibility. In every training, groups quickly names hypocrisy as one of the first examples of a bad supervisor. They fire off example after example, particularly around job performance, schedules, and accountability with time, of supervisors who operated by a different set of rules and adhered to a different set of standards from the rest of the team.

When your team can trust there will be consistency, they will trust you. They will trust that you are invested in keeping it equal, so they will trust you when you take corrective action, even if that action is with them.

How can you work to build a solid and stable climate and culture to support the success of your team? The Castle of Consistency model can be a helpful framework to explore where things are working, and where you may want to focus or expand your efforts.

❷ Castle of Consistency

Action: Castle of Consistency

Examine the messages you are sending to send to staff. Are the same norms/rules, expectations and standards consistently applied to all staff? Do they also apply to you? Pay close attention to challenging/sensitive areas, or places where there may have been issues with the staff/team in the past. What happened, and why did it happen?

Define: What

What kind of solid, stable, strong environment do you want to create for your team? Specifically name policies, procedures, protocols, standards, norms, climate/culture expectations you will have for all team members, including you.

- What is your specific, concrete and measurable goal? (How much, how many, by when?)
- What would having this mean for you, or do for you?
- What is of value to you about that goal?
- What does your goal look like when you've reached it, or how will you know you have reached it?

Clarify: Why

Why is it important for you to create a solid, stable, strong environment? Why does it matter to you that the team feels like they are treated equally and that you are consistent and fair with everyone?

- Why are you invested in reaching your goal?
- Why do you feel a sense of passion, commitment or alignment around this goal?
- Why is this goal a priority for you?
- Why would reaching this goal be of value to you, your work, your life?

Implement: How

How will you make this happen? How will you make the changes necessary to create the workplace you described? How will you take action and involve/include others in this initiative?

- How will you develop a plan and timeline for reaching this goal?
- How will you know you have achieved your goal?
- How will you address any barriers, challenges or obstacles?
- How/to whom will you be accountable?

Castle of Consistency

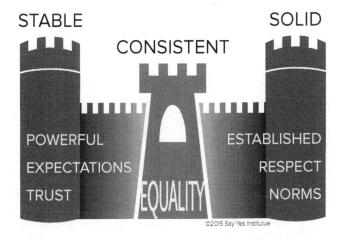

©2015 Say Yes Institutue

③ Know the Goal to Win the Game: Power of Clear Expectations

"I think about my goals when they are bigger, like a large project or event, but not when I head in to meetings or supervision. I never thought about that before." –Director

Before any meeting, conversation, interaction or supervision, do you take a moment to get clear on what you hope to accomplish in the exchange? Do you have a clearly named and defined goal? Perhaps a better question would be, did you even know you should have a goal?! If you are like most people you are blazing from one meeting to the next, one conversation to the next, without a second to think about what you're trying to do (or get, or learn, or cover), never mind figuring out whether or not you accomplished it!

As a leader, a lot is missing if you are moving through your days with an overall absence of clarity. It's absolutely absurd to think that you could end your day thinking about the accomplishments and successes if you've never taken the time to name what an accomplishment or success would even look like.

Here's another way to think about this: If you headed out on to the field and saw a pile of sports equipment and were told to, "Go win the game!" you would be confused. People want you to win, and you certainly want to win, but what should you do? Should you kick a ball, throw a ball, or make a basket? Are you playing alone, with a team, or with a partner? Obviously you want to do your best, and do what's right, but what are you trying to do? How could you ever strategize a plan to win if you never identified what you're trying to accomplish?

You could be thinking, "Well that's just absurd! Of course I wouldn't make any moves on the field or the court until I knew what I was trying to do!" That is logical. Nobody would make a move until they knew what the goal was, but this strategy actually still applies once we leave the equipment behind and head in to the office.

Can you imagine the impact of having clear goals, objectives and expectations in the office? Take a minute and imagine what would happen in your managing/supervising, or meetings, or trainings or conference calls if you took a minute before you started to get clear and asked yourself, "What is my goal in this situation? What am I trying to do?" There is no doubt the workplace would be a different place if people spent more time on the front end getting clear on goals, so they could spend less time on the back end doing damage control and putting out fires.

The power of clarity gives you the pause you need be in control of your thoughts and actions. It gives you the power that comes with focus and helps to shift your mood, direct your energy, and set your intention. It increases the likelihood that you will achieve your goal and meet your objective. It makes you thoughtful and clear. Bottom line, taking a minute to name your goal will put you ahead of the masses, since this is something that nobody seems to be doing as evidenced by the amount of energy people spend on damage control at work.

If you walk on the field or court you won't start playing full force until you know what the goal is, because you know you want to do your best. Implement that same level of clarity and focus as a manager in all of your interactions with the team. When you do, take notice of how powerful you feel, how other people respond to that power, and the endless number of "wins" filling your days!

③ Know the Goal to Win the Game

Action: Know the Goal to Win the Game

Think about interactions with members of your team (meetings supervision/training etc.) How have you prepared for those exchanges in the past? How has it worked for you? Can you think about times that you did not have a goal, and how that impacted the exchange? What about times when you did have a goal, what was the difference?

Define: What

What goals do you want to set around your interactions, meetings, supervisions etc.? What kind of "win" would you get from setting goals?

- What is your specific, concrete and measurable goal? (How much, how many, by when?)
- What would having this mean for you, or do for you?
- What is of value to you about that goal?
- What does your goal look like when you've reached it, or how will you know you have reached it?

Clarify: Why

Why is it important to you to have goals before you enter in to a conversation or meeting? Why will you/your team benefit from this level of goal setting and intentional clarity?

- Why are you invested in reaching your goal?
- Why do you feel a sense of passion, commitment or alignment around this goal?
- Why is this goal a priority for you?
- Why would reaching this goal be of value to you, your work, your life?

Implement: How

How will you start to apply the strategies of *Know the Goal to Win the Game* in your daily interactions with your team?

- How will you develop a plan and timeline for reaching this goal?
- How will you know you have achieved your goal?
- How will you address any barriers, challenges or obstacles?
- How/to whom will you be accountable?

❹ Communicate to Completion: Power of Effective Communication

"A simple communication exchange didn't go well and the fall out from that cost this department countless staff hours and thousands of dollars. People say they don't have time to communicate well, and I'm going to say that you better make time, because you're going to pay a lot more if you don't take the time!" –Manager

Most people spend a significant portion of each day in some kind of state of communication, meaning every single day we are all involved in countless communication exchanges. Some exchanges are benign, with minor or minimal impact on our lives if they don't go well, while others are quite significant, with the potential for extensive trauma or drama if there is a communication miss. With all the communication we are busy engaged in it may come as a surprise that most of our communication would actually be considered partial or incomplete communication—and at significant risk for going awry!

What constitutes partial or incomplete communication? It means that for most of us, after we say, type, or text our message-, whatever our message may be, then we consider the exchange done. We literally or figuratively walk away. We assume we clearly said it, and the other party understood what we meant, and what we want/need them to do with our message. If we even bother to take the time to ask the other person if they "got it," they will nod or say, "yeah," so then we are absolutely certain it was a success. We had something to say, we said it nice and clear, and we feel pretty good about doing our part in the communication dance. If there is any confusion, or the communication goes tragically awry, then it is obviously was not our fault. Any miscommunication or subsequent problems would be obviously attributed to the ineptitude of the other party, because we clearly did our part.

Bad news: Every communication exchange involves both parties until the end.

In training when we talk about this people are surprised (and sometimes angry) to hear when things go awry with communication there is never one innocent party and one guilty party. Both parties are equally responsible for what happens, or perhaps more importantly *doesn't* happen, with communication. There are many people walking around proudly proclaiming to be great communicators, but unfortunately the reality is for most people daily communication is not a success. Effective communication doesn't have to be a game of hit or miss anymore because there is something you can do to ensure what you said is what is heard, and what you mean is what is understood. This strategy will not only increase your communication success rate but it also will reduce conflict, build positive relationships, and expand productivity.

Most people are very interested to learn a specific strategy which will increase successful communication because most people have lived through the nightmare the comes form bad communication. The missing link in communication actually comes from moving the "finish line" with your communication exchange. Communication doesn't end when you're done with your message. Communicate to completion happens when you have received explicit confirmation the other person has heard and understood your message. This means you are not done, and this isn't over, until you know the other person understands what you have said. This is the single most important thing you can do to alleviate misunderstandings, reduce conflict, and minimize drama.

When you communicate to completion, you're making sure there is feedback coming back to you about what this person understands or will do. Another way to think about this is—you don't just throw the ball and walk away, do you? No. You know you aren't done until you make sure someone caught it. This is a significant shift for people, because we are used to just tossing the ball and walking away, assuming someone caught it. With that being said, this doesn't solely put responsibility on the person who threw the ball, because the person that is catching the ball in on the hook too. If someone throws you a ball you are now in this. It doesn't matter if you wanted to play or not, you're in it now. Both parties are responsible success. This new approach takes practice and commitment to consistently apply the strategy, but it works. If you use it, it will unequivocally work with an almost guaranteed success rate

Almost all conflict comes from a communication breakdown. It's not with malintent that things unravel, and it's not because people don't care, or they seek our or enjoy conflict. Communication is not a seamless process because we all don't share a brain, or universal frame of reference, or a standardized database of implicit/explicit meaning. We are all different so we interpret experiences and ascribe meaning differently. It is imperative for you to take time to make sure that people understand what you're saying, especially as a leader. When you are in charge it's crucial for you to foster and maintain a climate committed to clear, effective, and productive communication.

As supervisors, a lot of times we hit the ground running and assume people are with us. We think that they get it, and they're clear. Sometimes we say some version of, "so, you understand?" or maybe, "are we clear on this?" or perhaps we just say, "Got it?" To which the employee always says, "Yup!" Off you both go, only to find out next Tuesday, when the report is due, that they actually did not understand what you meant. Or maybe you find out when they don't show up for the shift that was changed. Or, perhaps it becomes evident when there is a crisis exploding on a Friday afternoon and you realize that the message that you thought they understood wasn't clear after all. That misconstrued memo dances to the tune of 127 hours of staff time to rectify the misunderstanding, translating to thousands of wasted dollars and many sleepless nights on your end.

How do you close the communication loop? Quite simply, you ask for feedback. You need to know before the meeting/supervision/training/conversation is over, what did the employee understand? What did they "get" from that exchange? What will they do? What will happen? When will it happen? How will there be follow up or check-in's? It's not in a condescending way ("What did I just say? Repeat it back."), it's more in the spirit of, "Let's recap and as we wrap up make sure we're all on the same page. What's happening next? What are you doing, and how will we follow up?"

This is actually a great conversation to have as a larger group, because it helps people understand a new shared norm around communication. It's not the responsibility of one person in a communication exchange to make sure this happens. It's on both ends, so similar to the ball being thrown and both parties being responsible for a successful catch, whether you're saying it, or it's being said to you, there should be a closing summary before walking away. People like to assume if there is any miscommunication that it was on the other party, because it certainly couldn't be that their initial message was unclear. On the other hand, people also assume if someone says something unclear to them, then it's not their problem if they didn't get it. Unfortunately the clarity of any message, in any exchange, is on both parties to own. Shifting the accountability to now apply to both parties to ensure success, not just sitting with the sender or receiver, helps increase the chances of closing the communication loop.

This means that even if you didn't want to be involved, didn't like the content, didn't understand the purpose, didn't have interest in any of the material shared, if someone says something to you, you are both in it now. Whether you said it, or it's said to you, be professional and make sure that you're clear before you walk away because the exchange isn't over until things have been clarified and confirmed. It's on both of you to make it work, because it will be on both of you if or when it doesn't! It's amazing how well this tool works, if you take the time to actually do it.

④ Communicate to Completion

Action: Communicate to Completion

- Think about your communication with your team. Where is it successful and where do you think it can it be improved?
- Has there ever been a time when communication did not go the way you wanted, or was not clear, or successful, or effective?
- What happened? Where was the breakdown?
- Would this situation have turned out differently if you had asked for feedback on the front end?

Define: What

What is your communication goal? What will you do to make sure you communicate to completion? What settings/situations do you want to focus on?

- What is your specific, concrete and measurable goal? (How much, how many, by when?)
- What would having this mean for you, or do for you?
- What is of value to you about that goal?
- What does your goal look like when you've reached it, or how will you know you have reached it?

Clarify: Why

Why is it important for you to communicate effectively?

- Why are you invested in reaching your goal?
- Why do you feel a sense of passion, commitment or alignment around this goal?
- Why is this goal a priority for you?
- Why would reaching this goal be of value to you, your work, your life?

Implement: How

How will you develop a concrete action plan on your new communication strategy?

- How will you develop a plan and timeline for reaching this goal?
- How will you know you have achieved your goal?
- How will you address any barriers, challenges or obstacles?
- How/to whom will you be accountable?

It's only a thought and a thought can be changed.

–Louise Hay

CHAPTER

5

Positive: LIKE

The positive is an energy boost and the negative is an energy drain. Read that one again. A simple concept with the capacity to be a catalyst to shift how you move through the world.

If that statement is accurate, what are the implications for you, your team, your work? Understanding the far-reaching impact of what that implies, on all levels, could be the biggest motivation for every leader out there to figure out ways to capitalize on the positive. If the positive is an energy boost, how does this increased energy impact a team? What is the impact on motivation? Morale? Investment? Productivity? Relationships and workplace dynamics? Play it out. What happens to a team, department, agency, business or bottom line when all of those areas have an infusion of energy? As a leader you know a lot happens, and all of it is good.

Understanding that a climate/culture focused on the positive creates energy, which benefits so many layers of the workplace, it suddenly makes the positive a high priority for leaders. Even leaders that aren't interested in traditional or typical "feel good" strategies suddenly begin paying attention to this connection to energy, because more energy leads to more of everything. More productivity. More success. More growth. More movement. More investment. More participation. More excitement. More alliance from staff. More money. Have you ever heard a leader say they didn't care about those things? The universal goals, of every great leader, are to inspire a team to achieve "more," on every level.

The infusion of energy which accompanies the positive is just as strong in the other direction when you flip to the negative. The negative is the greatest energy drain leaders will face with a team. A focus on the negative translates to a workplace void of energy, spark, passion, or motivation. People aren't connected and because of that lack of connection the team doesn't do much, and what they are doing, they're not doing well. The negative actually leads to "more" as well, but it's more of all of the things you don't want. More apathy, more complaining, and more conflict. The negative breeds more struggles, an increased lack of trust, and high turnover. Clearly, the negative is toxic, so it is safe to assume if you are leading a group you are invested in the positive because there is a big payoff for you, your team, and the bottom line.

For many people, finding and naming the positive in the world is a significant shift from the traditional focus they grew up with, which is typically centered on what went wrong. In many ways we are a deficit-based culture and we're skilled at noticing and naming what we don't like. We always seem to make time to share negative experiences. We are taught to address what is wrong, what isn't working, what didn't get done, didn't go well, didn't happen, or didn't make us happy. People will tell you how busy they are, yet in the midst of their busy lives they somehow always manage to find time to complain.

We feel comfortable finding mangers in stores and restaurants to make sure they are aware of the rude employee, cold chicken, or dirty glass on the table. We ask to see the manger whenever our feathers are ruffled, and all managers know it. Watch their body language as you approach; it's as if they are bracing themselves for the expected torrent of hostility and anger the public regularly bestows on them. If someone wants to talk to them then chances are inordinately high it's because something is wrong. It's unfortunate we are so predictable.

We complain in person, on the phone, online, and through social networks. Many of us are proficient at finding and sharing our dissatisfaction and take great pride in making the world aware of it. Notice how many people in social settings solely focus on the litany of negative experiences they have endured. They cover all that is wrong in their world when they are out to lunch, out with friends, over dinner, on a Friday night, or away on vacation. It's all about what went wrong, or who did something wrong. The focus on the negative is significant because it impacts a person's mood, outlook, feelings, and beliefs. Take note of how negative people report feeling physically because you don't need to be a doctor to observe some interesting patterns. Turns out on every level, mentally, emotionally, and physically, it feels bad to be grounded in the negative.

If the negative has such a profound impact on our thoughts, feelings, attitudes, moods, and outlooks, what does that mean about the positive? Exactly the same thing, except the positive has a significant impact in the other direction. It feels good to look for and name what is right with people, experiences, and the world. Mentally, physically, and emotionally there is value in finding and focusing on the positive. The powerful impact of a positive focus permeates mood, outlook, feelings, beliefs, and serves as a catalyst to shift one's entire experience of life. After working with thousands of people of all ages there has never been a single example of there being too much positive in someone's life. Nobody has ever said, "You know what I regret the most? Being positive about... (a person, or job, or situation, or event) because the negative would have been better." Not once has anyone said a focus on the positive side was a disappointment or a mistake.

How can you expand your capacity to find and name the positive, not just at work, but in your world? It's how you move through your days, every day, and what lens you use to filter your experiences. Have you ever called over the manger to appreciate and acknowledge a fabulous experience at a store or restaurant? Have you written a letter, made a phone call, tweeted or Facebooked about a positive experience, interaction, or exchange? "Why, yes I have!" some of you may say with glee, and proceed to point out that time, six years ago, when you did just that. Many have said they "thought about it" or "wanted to" but, they didn't. It's great that it crossed your mind, or that you actually did it once or twice, but imagine making it part of your day, every day?

What would the impact be if you made the positive a foundational part of your world? Could you build in a plan to actively seek out the positive, the successes, and the great moments that deserve a spotlight of recognition and appreciation? Another angle could be, if you were to receive a cash bonus every time you found and named a positive in your world, how much would you collect at the end of the day? The month? The year? You would be a millionaire, wouldn't you? You would look for the positive, find it everywhere, name it proudly, and celebrate it with glee! How would this shift how you move through your days? The positive is everywhere, and it is begging for you to take notice of it. If you start doing this you won't be getting cash, but you will be getting something even more valuable for your efforts. Your relationships, health, mood, work, home, and overall experience of life will benefit from this new positive lens. There is no downside, and no catch. The positive works in a big way, but most people don't use it.

As a leader, can you model what it looks like to move through this world with a tilt towards the positive? The benefits are endless for you, your team, and the work you will do together.

Action: Assessing the Positive
*Do you look for and find the positive in people,
performances, and projects?*

Think about how you find and name the positive in your life.

Where do you, or could you, find, name and celebrate the positive:

- About you?
- At work?
- In daily life?

Hint: Think about what is working, what you appreciate, what you feel grateful for, what you love, what you value, what bring you joy peace/contentment in the areas above.

Notice how you feel when you focus on the positive.

It shifts your energy, alters your mood, and fundamentally shifts your world view.

The positive is powerful, so use it!

Are you wondering, "What does this have to do with being the boss?" It has everything to do with it! If your lens is focused only on pointing out/ noticing the negative, that transfers to work. If you move through your days missing what went well, because you are focused on finding and addressing what did not go well, that transfers to work. Maybe you are someone that doesn't point out the negative or the positive, because you can't be bothered with any of it. That will come across at work as well.

As a leader it is important for you to be dialed in to the impact your focus and energy, positive or negative, has on your team. It is also key for you to understand if you choose to consistently and consciously focus on the positive, there is an immediate benefit to your team. People quickly learn you are a leader who takes notice of the positive. You not only notice the positive, you recognize it, and you celebrate it! Leaders often forget the impact they have on people by what they say/don't say and by what they do/don't do. There are a lot of people in leadership roles choosing to make that impact a positive one, and it is making a difference in so many lives.

Here are four tools/strategies to help you become a more Positive leader:

 ### The Positive Promise:
Change Your Lens, Change Your World

I know that I do better, and I feel better, when my attention on the positive, but I honestly don't always remember that angle when working with my team." –Team Leader

How can you check to see if things are focused on the positive at work? It's important to assess overall policies, norms, structure, and language. Think about meetings, projects, evaluations, and supervision. Where is the spotlight? It is on what is right and what is working? Is it on highlights, successes, and growth? Is it about validation, recognition, and appreciation? Or is your typical focus centered on what went wrong?

It is interesting to see how many people have meetings to primarily focus on and process what didn't happen, didn't work, or didn't go well. It's not a bad thing to explore what went awry, because it's necessary to learn and grow, but shining the light on the negative doesn't typically serve as a catalyst to launch people forward. Remember, the negative is an energy drain. Often people focus on all the problems, deplete the collective energy tank to zero, then ask the group to come up with excited, inspired, innovative ideas to address the issues and solve the problems. They seem puzzled and befuddled to find the team flat, disconnected, disinterested, and disengaged.

It's fascinating to watch because once the negative is addressed, and the room is filled with people in an apathetic and uninspired state, they then ask the group, "So people, what can we do differently next time? How can you make this better, or make sure that what went wrong won't go wrong again?" What do you think happens then? Exactly. Nothing!

There aren't any new angles or new ideas because the energy has been drained! So many people regularly do this. Maybe you are realizing you have even done it in the past with your team. Is it a surprise to see people don't have energy and excitement after they've been drowning in what went wrong and where they failed?

If you want people to be engaged, invested, excited and fully participate as they collectively plan how to go to the next level, ask them where they have succeeded, and how they plan doing or achieving more as they go forward.

You want to see a group explode? Focus on the positive, what is amazing, and what they are excited about. Feel the energy soar, and then from that place, ask the group where they can grow/expand/improve. They will innately address all of the missing pieces, broken parts, and unconnected dots as they eagerly plan next steps. The ownership and excitement is magical. Using this approach to group facilitation makes sense, yet it's amazing to see how new this is for so many leaders.

As you apply this concept to your team in a concrete way, what could it look like? You could start the team meeting/supervision with some kind of combination of, "Let's look at what worked. Where did we hit it out of the park? Where were you impressed with how we did? What were some of the highlights? Where do you feel you were successful?" This gets the energy up. This makes people feel good, as it should, and serves to shine the light on what worked and what went well.

Next ask what they could do to make it better or improve it for next time. Smiling and sparkling, they will not only tell you in general what improvements could be made, but they will also tell you what they can and will do to make it better, and how to successfully work together to improve things in the future. When you focus on the positive it works wonders, but when your team focuses on the positive, it is magic.

In order to focus on the positive it requires you to have some level of investment in finding the positive. You can't focus on something you don't see. The Positive Promise is a tool to help people see the steps they can take to build a solid positive foundation. The Positive Promise works because it is simple; easy to understand, easy to remember, and easy to use.

THE **POSITIVE** PROMISE
change your lens. change your world.

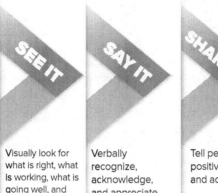

SEE IT

Visually look for what is right, what is working, what is going well, and what is gettting done.

SAY IT

Verbally recognize, acknowledge, and appreciate the positive.

SHARE IT

Tell people about the positive you observed and acknowledged.

(Bonus: make sure the person/group hears you share the positive with the boss, manager, parent coach, teacher, etc.)

©2015 Say Yes Institutue

This is my favorite model. Of everything I have done with people around building people skills, this model has consistently generated the most incredible feedback. The kind of feedback which gives chills and tears, because it is that good. When people head out in the world and they follow the steps of the Positive Promise and they *See It, Say It, Share It*, magic happens. Hearing about that magic is the most rewarding part of doing this work with people, because this is the stuff that changes lives. It changes how people look at the world and the people in it in the most profound way.

The first part of The Positive Promise asks people if they notice the positive in the world. Do they even see it, because not everyone does. If they do see it, which overwhelmingly most people will say they do, then the next question is, do they ever say anything to the person about it? Do they ever take the time to let the person know they noticed, or appreciated it, or valued what they said/did? Typically the room will be split on this one, with half saying they absolutely do this, and the other half saying they don't do this part as much as they could. The real deterioration in numbers comes when people are asked the last question, do they ever share this positive feedback with someone that would matter to this person? This means after you let the cashier know how helpful he was, do you find his manager and let her know this too (preferably with him being able to hear the positive gushing)? If you told a coworker how helpful she was, do you also send an email to the boss, cc'ing your coworker so she can see it as well? As you move through your days, do you *See* the positive, do you *Say* something when you see it, and then do you *Share* it?

The Positive Promise is a model every leader would benefit from using on a regular basis, as it serves as a reminder the focus of the leader matters—and there can never be too much positive at work, or in the world!

❶ The Positive Promise

Action: The Positive Promise

If the positive is an energy boost and the negative is an energy drain, take inventory and reflect on your focus and your energy at work. Where has it been? Where do you want it to be? How do you/can you use the positive with your team?

Define: What

What type of workplace do you want to create and maintain? What do you want it to look like, be like, feel like? What will you choose to focus on, and how will your focus contribute to building a strength-based climate/culture and a positive environment?

- What is your specific, concrete and measurable goal?
- (How much, how many, by when?)
- What would having this mean for you, or do for you?
- What is of value to you about that goal?
- What does your goal look like when you've reached it, or how will you know you have reached it?

Clarify: Why

Why is it important for you to focus on building the positive? Why are you interested in the impact the positive could have on the team?

- Why are you invested in reaching your goal?
- Why do you feel a sense of passion, commitment or alignment around this goal?
- Why is this goal a priority for you?
- Why would reaching this goal be of value to you, your work, your life?

Implement: How

How will you take action steps to bring the positive in to your daily world? How will you do things differently around noticing and acknowledging the positive?

- How will you develop a plan and timeline for reaching this goal?
- How will you know you have achieved your goal?
- How will you address any barriers, challenges or obstacles?
- How/to whom will you be accountable?

---

2 **Fill Your Well:**
You can't give what you don't have!

"I am stressed and overwhelmed and feel like I'm running on empty. It's like I have nothing left to give staff. I know they need more from me, but I just don't have it in me." –Manager

We have established it matters if the leader is positive, and it makes a significant impact on the whole team when a leader can see, and name, what is working. We are covering how to be positive in the world and positive with your staff/team. We are exploring how you can fully own the power that comes with being positive, and how you can use that power to shift how you move through you daily life. At this point you are on board and feeling excited about fully embracing your newfound passion for all things positive, except under that enthusiasm is a little bit of doubt because you are actually wondering who can maintain this state in daily life or in the "real world."

Being positive can feel like a lot of work, and some complain it is too hard to see what's right, when it's clear so much is wrong. Who are these people who are able to consistently embrace the upside of people, experiences, and life? Positive people are not living perfect lives, filled with endless moments of unadulterated bliss. These are not people dealt a better hand in life, or simpletons living simple lives void of any struggles, challenges, trauma, or drama. Positive people are living the same diverse life experiences as everyone else, yet they somehow manage to feel varying degrees of positive emotions on a regular and consistent basis. They are often described as being strong, happy, fulfilled, content, peaceful, calm, healthy, connected, joyful, optimistic, energetic, engaged, loving, grateful, and present. They aren't living perfect lives, but they do a great job finding and focusing on what is right, even when some things may be wrong.

Where do they get all of the energy to keep showing up in the world to find and name the positive? And what does this have to do with managing people? It has everything to do with it. You cannot give what you do not have. If you are running on empty and living in a depleted, burnt out, exhausted, stressed, overwhelmed, overloaded, and drained state, then you are not in a position to be harnessing the power of the positive with your team. You will not see what is right, what is going well, and what is getting done if you have nothing inside because you simply can not get water from an empty, dry well.

Let's talk about wells. How does a well work? A well can consistently gives out water because it is designed with a continuous supply of water coming in to the well, so there can be a continuous supply of water going out of the well. In one respect we are a lot like a well; we continuously give a lot, day in and day out. Unfortunately we are missing the other crucial piece of the well, as people do not have a continuous source of refueling, refilling, replenishing happening in their daily lives. After asking countless people, "what fills your well?" it became tragically clear we have a crisis happening out there around self-care because there are a lot of empty, dry, and dusty wells in our midst!

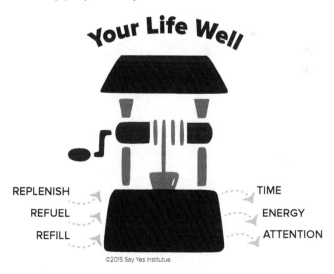

Your Life Well

REPLENISH
REFUEL
REFILL

TIME
ENERGY
ATTENTION

©2015 Say Yes Institutue

Your Life Well was created to help people visually see the importance of making time for what refuels, refills, or replenishes them, or else the well runs dry. This model is not something specific to one type of person, or one kind of industry. This tool can be universally applied and the goal is to help people look at self-care through a different lens. This is not an optional and decadent indulgence. This is the foundation to who you are and how you are able to move through this world.

ACTIVITY
Taking inventory of Your Life Well

Directions:

Step One: Draw Your Life Well on a piece of paper.

Step Two: Where does your time/energy/attention go? Draw arrows coming out of Your Life Well and name those things. These are not negative, and this is not a bad thing, it is to show you where you spend your valuable time, energy, and attention.

Step Three: What replenishes, refuels, refills you? Draw arrows coming in to Your Life Well and name what nourishes you. These should not be things that require a lot of time or money (a vacation next year doesn't count!); these are things that you can do every day. You may not necessarily be doing them all right now, but it's important for you to know what they are. Can you come up with at least 10 things with the ability to fill Your Life Well? Can you come up with more than 10?

Step Four: Take inventory of what is going out, and what is coming in. Are you doing enough to take care of yourself? When looking at Your Life Well most people find they need to do more to replenish, refuel, and refill the well. Can you commit to doing more of the things that refill Your Life Well? What will you do within the next day? Can you make a plan to keep filling Your Life Well on a daily basis?

People often say they simply "don't have time" to do anything to refill their well. They are busy, important people who do a lot, give a lot, are responsible for a lot, manage a lot, produce a lot etc., and they just can't spare a minute to do anything they view as being optional or elective. There is nothing optional or elective about filling one's well. When people do not take care of themselves and the well runs dry, the impact is significant.

When clients come in to coaching it is often with lists of perceived "problem areas" in life where they are struggling, and it quickly becomes clear for the majority of the people it comes down to an empty well. They are burnt out, stressed, exhausted, overwhelmed, overloaded, depressed, or empty. They share examples of struggles with family, friends, work, and their health. Whatever examples or descriptions they give, the bottom line is always the same; they haven't been taking care of themselves. People are often struck by how little comes in to their well, because they haven't made it a priority. If you are giving a lot every day, then you need daily filling. People, including managers and supervisors, are at their best when the well is full, or at least has a steady supply of some water coming in to it!

Your Life Well is important because everything you want to do, achieve, or accomplish as a leader starts with you. You bring you in to the office every day, thereby making you and how you feel a foundational part of this process. Again, you can't give what you don't have. As a leader it takes a lot of energy to focus on the positive, communicate effectively, support professional growth, maintain accountability, and hold the larger vision for the team. In order to do all of this, you must take care of you. That's the only way to do it, because that's the only way you *can* do it. In order to give a lot, you need to have a lot to give, so make sure you are filling Your Life Well.

Action: Fill Your Well

Take inventory on how you are feeling right now. Think about your physical state, in addition to your mental/emotional state. In general, would you say you feel calm, clear, focused, peaceful, powerful, productive, successful, positive, and in a good place with things? If that is not an accurate description, then how do you feel? Think about your work world, then go macro and think about your entire world. What words accurately capture how you feel?

Define: What

What did you notice about how you feel and Your Life Well? What are you doing to take care of you, so you have energy to bring to your team (and your life)? What do you want to do more of?

- What is your specific, concrete and measurable goal? (How much, how many, by when?)
- What would having this mean for you, or do for you?
- What is of value to you about that goal?
- What does your goal look like when you've reached it, or how will you know you have reached it?

Clarify: Why

Why is it important for you to spend time/energy on filling your well?

- Why are you invested in reaching your goal?
- Why do you feel a sense of passion, commitment or alignment around this goal?
- Why is this goal a priority for you?
- Why would reaching this goal be of value to you, your work, your life?

Implement: How

How will you take steps to start filling your well? How will you do things differently?

- How will you develop a plan and timeline for reaching this goal?
- How will you know you have achieved your goal?
- How will you address any barriers, challenges or obstacles?
- How/to whom will you be accountable?

3   Mental Ticker Tape:
Owning Your Thoughts

"I know it's important to be positive, and I think I'm saying the right things, but if people could see what I was thinking they would be horrified! If I had to be honest, I'm not really that optimistic about whether or not we can really do this (make changes)." –Director

A lot of people say they work really hard to be positive, and find what is right, what is working, and what is going well. They want to stay in the place where they can capitalize on the immense power that comes with positive energy and every day they want to do it, yet there are things getting in the way making it difficult for people to stay in that place. Do you know what the most common struggle is for people? It's something most people don't even know is happening, so they have no ability to address it. It's the mental ticker tape running nonstop in your head, and it's typically programmed with negative sentiments. Sentiments so negative it could appear as if it were operated by some kind of pessimistic, evil, horrid creature with the sole purpose of sabotaging your world as it negatively targets everyone and everything in your life. We have already established what the negative does to your mood and energy and it's not good, so we really should get a handle on this one!

For many people the Mental Ticker Tape is a new concept. We know a ticker tape is typically a black sign, with red writing running across the screen stating how much milk is, or what's on sale, or shares some kind of message/greeting or update. It runs the same message over and over, until someone changes the content. Do you have a visual?

Imagine that you have one of those in your head, which runs all day long with countless messages about your world and the people in it. This is not a phenomenon unique to you, as we all have it, and it's always running. We just aren't conscious of it, so we never examine the content for accuracy, meaning, or impact.

If you are in doubt that this applies to you, or questioning if you have an active Mental Ticker Tape, see if any of the following resonates for you...

Mental Ticker Tape: Heading in to supervision

Sally isn't going to have the report done. She never finishes anything. She is unreliable and irresponsible. Let's see what kind of excuses she comes up with today. I'm guessing she hasn't even started.

▓ Mental Ticker Tape: Heading in to team meeting

This team is unbelievable. I bet most of them did nothing, again. Claire and Tyson probably did it all and carried the ball for the team, like they always do. This team is a joke.

You don't even say anything out loud; you could just think it, and this thinking shapes your mood and your energy before you even utter a single word. The negative thoughts have set the tone for how your supervision will go, and how your team meeting will unfold. Again, most people are shocked to dial in to how often this happens because we are overwhelmingly unaware of our ongoing mental ticker tape. When people acknowledge it is happening they will quickly deny the impact this has on their outward interactions with others. Big mistake. On every level this shapes how you connect, relate, and engage with people around you.

Did you know the Mental Ticker Tape doesn't just run negative mental thoughts about other people; it actually runs endless streams of critical, negative, and less than kind statements about you too! See if any of these thoughts have ever whirled in your head...

▓ Mental Ticker Tape: Upcoming training

Train? What?! YOU?! Are you kidding? Last training you did was awful. What are you thinking? You're not good at this. What a stupid idea!

▓ Mental Ticker Tape: A raise

You're not getting a raise, so don't even bother. What have you even done this year? Forget it. You're not that good at what you do and they aren't giving you a dime more than you're getting, so stop dreaming. There isn't any money right now anyways so it won't happen. Don't waste your time.

Negative Mental Ticker Tape

I can't... It won't... They haven't...

©2015 Say Yes Institutue

Now take it out of the workplace, just to illustrate how the Mental Ticker Tape has the ability to permeate all parts of your life.

Mental Ticker Tape: Dating scene
He/she will never go out with you. Look at you. You're a mess. You can't just walk up to someone and ask them out like that because you look desperate. Nobody really does that. I bet s/he is already taken anyways.

Mental Ticker Tape: Getting healthy
Oh, please! You aren't going to go really go to a gym! You never follow through on anything you start. You can buy fruit, but you won't eat it. You fail at this every time—so why even bother? It's pointless and you'll never do it. You're lazy. Don't waste your money on a lost cause.

Does any of that sound familiar? Change the context, the players, the details, and do any of those read like they were lifted right out of your head? What is most concerning about this is the fact that this "mental ticker tape" is actually not being run by some kind of evil creature, set on ensuring your demise. What makes this so bizarre is the ticker tape is solely run and staffed around the clock, by you. Every day everything on it is what you put there. This is always a fun activity in trainings because people are mystified as to how this could have happened, and continues to happen, without their knowledge or consent.

If you want to stay positive, it's imperative that you are in charge of what you are saying, and thinking, on both a conscious as well as sub-conscious level. This means you are taking control of the conscious and intentional words you speak, as well as the subconscious and hidden beliefs you hold. Your Mental Ticker Tape can serve to be your greatest ally, supporting your positive thoughts, feelings, and actions, or it can be the biggest contributor to your self-sabotage. For most people just the awareness that they are running a Mental Ticker Tape is enough of a catalyst to shift the content to a more positive and productive flow.

Positive Mental Ticker Tape

I can... It will... They have...

©2015 Say Yes Institutue

Action: Control Your Mental Ticker Tape

You have a ticker tape running in your head, all the time. It has thoughts about you, your abilities, your performance, your value/worth etc., and it also has thoughts about everyone else around you. Are you aware of what your Mental Ticker Tape is saying? Take inventory to determine if the messages you are putting on your Mental Ticker Tape are contributing to your life, at home and at work? Assess the content you are running on your Mental Ticker Tape and decide if those messages are positively or negatively impacting your world.

Define: What

What messages do you want your ticker tape to say, about you and about the people in your world?

- What is your specific, concrete and measurable goal? (How much, how many, by when?)
- What would having this mean for you, or do for you?
- What is of value to you about that goal?
- What does your goal look like when you've reached it, or how will you know you have reached it?

Clarify: Why

Why is it important for you to take ownership of the content of your ticker tape?

- Why are you invested in reaching your goal?
- Why do you feel a sense of passion, commitment or alignment around this goal?
- Why is this goal a priority for you?
- Why would reaching this goal be of value to you, your work, your life?

Implement: How

How will you take ownership of the messages/content of your ticker tape? How will you take steps to change the content of your Mental Ticker Tape and run messages which contribute to your overall mood/state/outlook/perspective?

- How will you develop a plan and timeline for reaching this goal?
- How will you know you have achieved your goal?
- How will you address any barriers, challenges or obstacles?
- How/to whom will you be accountable?

**Other People's Stuff (OPS):
The Power of Ownership**

*"I can't tell you how many days I leave here feeling like they're in competition
for who has the biggest crisis happening in their lives. Everyone has a reason
why they can't do something, or didn't get something done. I'm tired of it
falling on me to do it all!" –Supervisor*

Do you want to know what positive people know? Do you want to know
how they are able to maintain a positive state, on a day to day basis? Not
a lot of people know this one, so pay attention.

They don't carry Other People's Stuff (OPS).

They don't carry, internalize, personalize, own, or take on other
people's issues, moods, struggles, challenges, problems, attitudes, hurts,
frustrations or anger. They move through the day able to simultaneously hold compassion for other people with an awareness they are never
responsible for fixing, curing, solving, rectifying, holding, owning, moving
or carrying anyone else's baggage. They refuse to be responsible for
carrying Other People's Stuff.

This may sound like something everyone should already know and
adhere to, but it's not. This concept is a mind-blowing new angle for a
lot of people. It is important to note even those who already know it are
still guilty of regularly carrying what isn't theirs to carry.

The fact is, everyone has stuff. We all go through life carrying varying
amounts of baggage from the past, as well as the continuous accumu-
lation that comes from just living daily life. Some are so adept at this
they have even mastered the art of accumulating baggage from possible
future actions or events they haven't even lived yet. The worry and an-
ticipation of what could go wrong in the future has the capacity to
produce baggage at the same rate as experiences already lived. It is quite
remarkable how many possible avenues one can accumulate stuff from.
With so many equally accessible options to accumulate our own baggage,
why does it seem some people are consistently accumulating so much
more than others? It's because they are carrying baggage from other
people.

Baggage is a given accompaniment of life and showing up and moving
through the world ensures you are going to be bumping in to a lot of
moods, emotions, and attitudes. On a daily basis it takes a very clear and
focused person to move through the world baggage free. Beyond the

challenge of not accumulating your own baggage, from your own experiences, there are people out there who are actively looking to dump their "stuff" and give their baggage to other people. In other words, if they aren't ok, they want to make sure you aren't ok either. Then there are people that just seem to seek out other people's issues, problems and struggles and happily take them on. Nobody forced them to take on drama, but these people intently hunt it down and pick it up with glee. Any pain they can scoop up becomes one more thing for them to complain about as they stockpile misery to eagerly share with any and all in their path.

There are lots of ways to pick up baggage; inadvertently, accidentally, or willingly. People need to take inventory on what they are lugging around through life. The first step is to determine if what you are carrying is yours or if it belongs to, or came from, someone else. If it is yours, is it adding anything to your life or your experience? You need to ask yourself if you want to continue carrying it. If it's not yours, where did you get it and why are you carrying it? What purpose is it serving you by continuing to lug around someone else's baggage? What benefits do you reap from carrying the pain, anger, frustration, or resentment from other people?

Part of being a leader can translate to people feeling a sense of responsibility or accountability for the struggles of people in his/her life. A lot of leaders are quick to take on or own a lot, which can morph in to them becoming a metaphorical dumping ground for the team, as well as other people in their lives. Holding and carrying excessive baggage leaves leaders feeling exhausted, depleted, stressed, frustrated, agitated, and overwhelmed.

You would never walk in to a coffee shop, or a store, or a meeting, and then leave with bags of "S*%$" from other people, would you? That would be disgusting and obscene. Nobody would ever, ever, EVER do that.

Yet we all do it every day with emotional baggage. Matter of fact, you have probably already done it many times today and just accept it as a normal part of life.

You do it.

Your team does it.

Your neighbors do it.

Your spouse does it.

Your sister does it.

Strangers do it.

If we aren't careful, or vigilant, it will happen countless times throughout the day, every day.

How do you know you are doing it? Someone else is angry and your chest constricts and blood pressure goes up. That means you just picked up a few of his/her "bags." You're in a meeting and you notice someone comes in agitated, and when the meeting's over now you are agitated too. Good news, you just left with a bag or two. You enter a store happy, then after an unpleasant interaction with a cashier you leave the store with an edge or an attitude, you just left with someone else's baggage. See how fast it happens?

Here's how OPS works:

❶ You are happy, content, fine, peaceful etc.

❷ You encounter a person who is upset or angry, agitated, frustrated, stressed etc.

❸ You walk away and now you feel angry, agitated, frustrated, and stressed.

What just happened? The person with the problem is gone, but the negativity is left behind. There you are, left holding his/her baggage, problems, anxieties, struggles, challenges, bad feelings, or bad moods. You are left with his/her "S*#&." The biggest piece is, you aren't just left there with it, you then carry it with you in to your day, from meeting to meeting, errand to errand, office to home, you move through the day carrying OPS!

Other People's Stuff: OPS

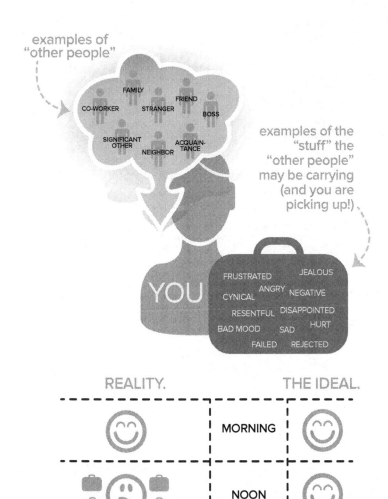

examples of "other people"

FAMILY
FRIEND
CO-WORKER
STRANGER
BOSS
SIGNIFICANT OTHER
NEIGHBOR
ACQUAINTANCE

examples of the "stuff" the "other people" may be carrying (and you are picking up!)

YOU

FRUSTRATED   JEALOUS
ANGRY   NEGATIVE
CYNICAL
RESENTFUL   DISAPPOINTED
BAD MOOD   SAD   HURT
FAILED   REJECTED

REALITY.		THE IDEAL.
🙂	MORNING	🙂
🧳🧳 ☹️ 🧳🧳	NOON	🙂
🧳🧳🧳 😠 🧳🧳🧳	NIGHT	🙂

A lot of us move through the world looking for, grabbing, picking up, and carrying OPS. As you move through the day you could start by transporting 2 bags, by lunch increase to 10 bags, then to 23 bags by afternoon, and end your day pulling in the driveway with 78 bags of OPS. Imagine transporting OPS with you throughout the day and exponentially increasing the amount as the day goes on. How does this impact you? What does this do to your mood, your outlook, your energy, your state of mind?

Now, what does this mean if you're the boss? People are going to come in to work carrying a lot of "stuff," but it isn't on you to handle or own any of it. Whatever negativity, bad moods, frustrations, disappointments, failures, anger, or sadness people are carrying, it is ultimately on them to manage themselves and engage appropriately at work. It's important to remember that even though people may be dealing with a lot, there is still an expectation if they show up for work then they will be able to work. They are being paid to do a job and regardless of how much baggage they are carrying, they are adults and it should be assumed they will handle themselves in a professional manner. As the boss you are there to encourage the professional growth and development of your team, not be a therapist or crisis counselor. You are there to support people, not fix people. You are there for your team, but you are not doing it for team. Be aware of how you support people, without taking on what isn't yours to carry, fix, deal with, or address.

How do you do this?
You ask yourself some questions:

- *How are you feeling?* Continuously check in with where you are at and how you feel before/after meetings, supervision, training, conversations etc. If you start out the day feeling pretty good, and end the day feeling like you've been steamrolled by life, it means during the day you were been very busy picking up and transporting OPS! Can you pinpoint where you seem to be picking up OPS? Most people have no idea how they are feeling, so they're oblivious as to when they got derailed.

- *What are you going to do?* Once you notice you have been negatively impacted by someone else's mood and you are carrying around OPS, you need to decide if it is helping you. Is it contributing to your day, your mood, your experience, or your life in a positive way? If it's not adding anything, do you want to keep doing it? What can you do differently going forward? Remember, if you don't have the power to control, or fix, or solve something, then it's not yours to carry!

How do you succeed with this one? It is imperative you are aware of what emotional state you're in and tune in to your thoughts/feelings on a regular basis. The reason most people succumb to carrying so much of OPS is because they are not paying attention to their moods/feelings. If you feel positive and you leave an interaction with a coworker/supervisee/family member/stranger and now you feel negative, agitated, or frustrated then it is possible you have just left with OPS. Was that your intention? Remember, if it isn't yours, it isn't yours to carry, so leave it behind!

④ Other People's Stuff (OPS)

Action: Stop Carrying OPS

Positive people do not have time, space or energy to carry Other People's Stuff. Think about your days at work and notice how you feel before, during and after you meet with or interact with the team. Your mood is the best indicator of whether you're carrying anyone else's baggage/issues/struggles/frustrations/stressors etc. To help you get clear on how you may be impacted by OPS, describe how you feel before, during, and after different meetings or exchanges. Do you notice any patterns?

Define: What

What is your goal around carrying Other People's Stuff?

- What is your specific, concrete and measurable goal? (How much, how many, by when?)
- What would having this mean for you, or do for you?
- What is of value to you about that goal?
- What does your goal look like when you've reached it, or how will you know you have reached it?

Clarify: Why

Why is it important for you to make changes around carrying Other People's Stuff?

- Why are you invested in reaching your goal?
- Why do you feel a sense of passion, commitment or alignment around this goal?
- Why is this goal a priority for you?
- Why would reaching this goal be of value to you, your work, your life?

Implement: How

How will you develop a plan to stop carrying Other People's Stuff? How will you leave meetings, supervisions, trainings, conference calls etc., with no baggage? How can you support your team to understand and implement this tool as well?

- How will you develop a plan and timeline for reaching this goal?
- How will you know you have achieved your goal?
- How will you address any barriers, challenges or obstacles?
- How/to whom will you be accountable?

Footnote on OPS: The purpose of this tool is to give you a possible perspective to help you move through your day without taking on the moods, frustrations, issues, or stressors from other people. A lot of people find this to be a powerful tool to help them reframe ownership and accountability, yet many struggle with the perception this may in some way mean they don't care about the struggles/challenges or "stuff" someone else is carrying. That is not the case.

The purpose of OPS is to understand you cannot successfully take on or take over someone else's baggage. The only thing you can do, if it's appropriate, is support someone to recognize they are carrying baggage, and let them decide if they think it makes sense for them to continue to do so or if they want to make a plan to let it go. You can care about someone, but it's not up to you to fix, solve, or eliminate their struggles, pain, or difficulties. The hope is the OPS model will help people understand the only person in a position to let go of baggage is the original owner.

I praise loudly.
I blame softly.

–Catherine the Great

CHAPTER

6

Professional: MODEL

ow important is it for a leader to be perceived as professional?
Of the three components of this book, the "professional" piece
could be the most interesting, because while not every leader
confidently owns the identity of being powerful or positive, I have yet
to meet a manager who did not claim to be professional. There appears
to be a universal expectation or assumption that a leadership role implies
one must innately embody what it means to be professional.

In countless workshops and training, "professional" is consistently
one of the top words managers/supervisors/leaders proudly used to
describe who they are, or how they are. It is logical to assume a leader
would consistently have the perception of being professional, simply
based on the nature of the position, yet this is an area which is actually
difficult for many people to master. It is not as easy, or as innate, as people
expect it to be, and it is certainly not a way of being which automatically accompanies a title. This is a skill, and like all skills, only improves with
time, energy and attention.

To successfully own what it means to be professional it is imperative
you are operating within an environment supporting a professional
culture and climate. A professional environment reflects policies, procedures and norms tied to the overall infrastructure and encompasses
evaluations, performance reviews, meetings, trainings, unrolling new
initiatives, or anything else that frames the structure of how the team

works, individually and/or collectively and collaboratively.

The easiest way to say this is if you are the leader, when you say something, or when you do something, make sure it is happening in a context that enables it to mean something.

"I don't know why they even bother—it's such a joke here. I do it the yearly Employee Evaluation the week before it's due, and then we never look at it again, until next year." –Supervisor

"You have no idea how much I dread supervision. I don't do it often, but when I do it's painful for both of us." –Team Leader

"It feels like we follow a 'flavor of the month' kind of structure here. Every new training leads us in a new direction, so nobody seems too invested in any new ideas anymore and nothing has ever taken off." – Director

If you're going to continue doing things which don't mean anything, wouldn't it be freeing, and fun, to just call it what it is? It could sound something like this:

"We are about to embark on another round of evaluations. We all know that this is an arbitrary and superfluous process that has no merit and/or connection to your work, your salary or your performance. You and I will proceed with little thought and no pretense of investment as we try to piece together, based on sketchy memory, some semblance of your past year of performance, which will clearly rely heavily on the past two months since that is all you and I are actually able to recall. We will then have an obligatory meeting where we will both muddle through attempting to appear as though we both have some vested interest around this profoundly inadequate assessment of your performance and future potential. We will both watch the clock, knowing that in one short hour it will be over and we will sign the form and return it, filled with upcoming goals and perfunctory ramblings of successes/challenges from the past year, to a file in a desk, where is shall remain safely undisturbed for the next 364 days. Please agree that you are complicit in this dirty little secret and we shall proceed, as planned, and as we have many times before. Sign here. Thank you for your time."

How refreshing would it be to just call it what it is, which is nothing.

The tragedy in the scenario above is the possibility that it doesn't have to be like that. What if performance evaluations could be reclaimed as a useful process to guide professional growth and development? Unfortunately, for so many places, it is not used to its full potential and doesn't add anything to the culture. There are so many workplaces which have developed infrastructures that actually provide valid, helpful or powerful tools, but they simply aren't used properly, appropriately, or consistently.

Beyond evaluations, supervision is another area that makes people cringe. So many supervisors and staff have consistently said, "What's the point of it? Why bother? It's a waste of time!"

It is a waste of time if it's sporadic, people are not prepared, or if there is no structure. It is a waste of time if it's merely a running report of what already was done, or consists of a supervisor rattling off a list of what tasks/projects need to be completed. If that's the case, why not just send a bulleted email and save you both that dreaded hour every week, or every month?

Supervision is an amazing opportunity to support staff development and growth. It is a chance for the supervisor to be pushed/challenged to find ways to support and motivate staff, while holding staff accountable for their professional performance and growth in a concrete and measurable way. There is immense power and possibility in the process of supervision, if you show up prepared and all parties are invested in it.

There are many examples of procedures, policies and protocols that are empty and hollow. Yearly performance evaluations and weekly/monthly supervision meetings are just two examples of a seemingly endless list of missed opportunities in the workplace. As a manager/supervisor, how can you revisit these pieces in order to create large scale credibility? Even if your larger climate/culture isn't jumping in with both feet on this one, is there a way you could increase the relevance around some of these areas, particularly with supervision and performance evaluations/reviews? Being professional means there is value and worth in what is being done in the office, and anything that is being done actually has meaning, otherwise you would not do it.

Be specific and concrete. Be sure to use positive language around what you want it to be, not about what you don't want it to be.

After exploring the larger context around how the infrastructure can contribute to or support a professional climate and culture, how you can take ownership around contributing to building a professional environment?

Here are three tools/strategies to help you become a more Professional leader:

1️⃣ Clear on Boundaries

"It was a big mistake to say anything about what I am dealing with around some financial issues, since I make significantly more than the staff. I wish I could take it back." –Vice President

"Biggest regret? That's an easy one. I went out with the team and they saw me drink too much. They even have pictures of it. It definitely impacted how they see me. In retrospect, I can't believe I did that and I am embarrassed by my behavior." –Director

"Nobody thinks boundaries are a big deal until they are crossed and things seem to fall apart. Leaders need to keep this on the radar all the time, but so many don't and it's unfortunate because you pay dearly for poor boundaries! Trust me!" –Executive Director

This topic can single-handedly undo one's aspiration to be professional. It can cause endless struggles, grief, and regret. It can sabotage the biggest and the best, sending the seemingly infallible in to the abyss of "what not to do." If you want to be revered for your stellar grasp on what it means to be professional, living as the kind of boss that you want to be, it is imperative you are clear on the importance of maintaining clear, healthy, and consistent boundaries in the workplace.

This is a tough area for people because most people have a powerful desire, whether they will admit it or not, to be liked. Even though they are in charge, leaders still have this urge to connect with the team and be considered part of the team. While the leader is capable of connecting and certainly can be in a position to be liked, the nature of the position of a leader precludes the capacity to ever fully assimilate in to the group. The role of the leader is to lead the group, so this absence of equality means there will never be reciprocity in this relationship, ensuring there will never be full acceptance in to a group. You cannot run the group while simultaneously holding an equal place in the group, although many have certainly led a valiant effort to prove this theory wrong. Lean from their misery. It cannot be done.

The unequal power balance in the relationship between a leader and the team renders the relationship a clearly defined, non-negotiable, one-way street. It can never be a two-way street because it is within the scope of your job to evaluate, write up, put on probation or terminate people. You have a say in salary, time off, promotions, and schedules. You have the capacity to impact the trajectory of someone's professional path, which means you have power over them. Leaders with the capacity to remember the importance of this power imbalance do very well. They understand the precarious balance of the position, and the need to always respect this dynamic by establishing and maintaining clear boundaries.

On the other side of this equation are leaders who disregard, forget, or ignore this power imbalance. They have ongoing issues, struggles, and challenges with the team. Refusing to acknowledge the "power over" angle wreaks havoc with teams, but it does a number on the leader as well. It is important to always remember the people you supervise are not your peers or your equals, so they are not your friends. The workplace is not where you "tell all" about your life. Here is a good benchmark for sharing: If it's something you wouldn't tell/show or share with a child, or the stranger in line behind you at the grocery store, then please do not tell/show or share it with the people you supervise. This means there is never a time that you should show how well you can hold your alcohol by demonstrating how many shots you can still do, nor should you feel inclined to share the sordid details of your dating life, your horrific divorce, or your escalating financial troubles.

You are there to support, encourage, inspire, and hold accountable. You are not there to make friends or be friends. People will argue against this with attempts to prove that they can walk that line with grace and ease, but it gets really hard to write someone up on Monday morning after they watched you stumble around in a drunken stupor Friday night. It doesn't sit well with people when they have heard you complain about your finances for months, knowing you make at least $45,000+ more than they do, then you tell them there is a freeze on raises and bonuses for the indefinite future. Your job titles certainly are not blurry; make sure your relationship boundary lines are not blurry either.

Some leaders will say they have things going on in life, and it's only natural to let the team know. There is a difference between letting people know a snippet of what is happening, like you are dealing with health issues with your mother, but another to use work as a platform to process your personal life. Many will say that would never happen, or wonder who would actually do that, but unfortunately it happens frequently. Those bad boundaries are doing damage on every level with leaders and teams. When leaders bring their issues/drama from life in to the workplace all it serves to do is erode their credibility and diminish their capacity to lead. You have friends, don't you? If you need to talk, talk to them. If you're going to go out, then go out with them, and focus on being a leader for your team.

The model below was developed to help people visualize the difference in the two kinds of boundaries. It's helpful to illustrate the line between the two to solidify the importance of being clear on how boundaries shift as relationships shift; all relationships are not created equal.

Understanding Boundaries

Power: Neutral

Peers/Equals
Friends
Colleagues
Family

Mutual
Shared
Balanced
Equal
Reciprocal

Power: Imbalance

BOSS/Employee
STAFF/Client
PARENT/Child

Encourage
Support
Inspire
Lead
Motivate

©2015 Say Yes Institutue

---

❶ Boundaries

Action: Set Better Boundaries

Reflect on your boundaries with different people in your world. Think about relationships in your personal life (friends, family, neighbors, acquaintances), then think about professional relationships. How would you categorize the power you hold in those relationships? What relationships have neutral/equal power, and where is the power balance unequal? Why is it important to be aware of boundaries? What is the impact?

Define: What

What kind of boundaries do you want to have as a leader? What does it look like for you to consistently maintain professional boundaries? What will you do/not do?

- What is your specific, concrete and measurable goal? (How much, how many, by when?)
- What would having this mean for you, or do for you?
- What is of value to you about that goal?
- What does your goal look like when you've reached it, or how will you know you have reached it?

1 Boundaries
Clarify: Why
Why do you want to create and maintain professional boundaries with your team? Why does this matter?
• Why are you invested in reaching your goal?
• Why do you feel a sense of passion, commitment or alignment around this goal?
• Why is this goal a priority for you?
• Why would reaching this goal be of value to you, your work, your life?
Implement: How
How will you develop and maintain professional boundaries with your team? How will take steps and do things differently in order to ensure you are consistently able to fulfill your commitment to this goal?
• How will you develop a plan and timeline for reaching this goal?
• How will you know you have achieved your goal?
• How will you address any barriers, challenges or obstacles?
• How/to whom will you be accountable?

2 Clear on Ownership

"Every meeting it seems like I am telling them over and over that they need to take initiative, take a lead, take ownership and every meeting they look back at me with blank stares. It's getting so old and I don't know how else to say it!" –Associate Director

"All I will say is the level of apathy here is toxic. I'm not sure why, but it is. I'm throwing my hands up on this one." –Unit Manager

"I dread running meetings here. I've never seen a group like this. Nobody seems to say a thing, except for me. I keep presenting ideas but they never go anywhere." –Manager

We have established it is important to support professionalism through the infrastructure in place around policies/procedures etc., as well as by leaders having clear boundaries. The next level of professionalism expands to focus on how the leader develops the participation, or ownership, of the team. How do you ensure people are actively engaged, individually and collectively, on every level? How do you develop ownership around goals, initiatives, projects, vision, mission, and future growth?

Leaders seem to be consistently struggling with this piece and many report feeling like no matter how many times they say it's important, or how much they want or need people to take initiative and ownership, nothing happens. Why is it so complicated? Why do so many managers complain about this piece? Are there just a lot of leaders that got a bad hand and were dealt a lazy, disconnected, and apathetic team?

The good news is it's not a flawed team, it's just a flawed approach. Leaders need to revisit the strategy they are using to engage the team and build ownership. They need to remember nobody is ever going own something s/he did not put anything IN to. People need to contribute something to the process in order to ever own the process.

People think you can expect, demand, or mandate ownership. You can certainly expect, demand, or mandate that people complete tasks, perform duties, and maintain perfunctory participation, but if you want authentic, engaged, electric, inspired, and incredible participation that comes with owning something, you need to give people the opportunity to put something in! The Ownership Model helps illustrate the process of how to shift a culture/climate to become more engaged and participatory.

Ownership Model

©2015 Say Yes Institutue

The Ownership Model was created to help leaders understand the importance of the process of involvement is to creating ownership. It illustrates how the catalyst for supporting ownership originates from Input. Input provides people with the opportunity to share their thoughts, feelings, experiences, suggestions, and insights.

This Input immediately translates to an increased Interest in what is happening, how it is happening, and when it is happening. As that Interest builds, there is a natural and authentic Investment in to the process. That Investment leads to the desire to have additional Input, which leads to an ever expanding Interest and fully engaged Investment. What develops as that cycle goes around and around? A genuine, engaged, electric Ownership! When people are engaged and put something IN to the process, it expands and becomes internalized as the elusive state of Ownership so many leaders crave.

You can tell, or yell, or demand ownership, but you aren't going to ever get it that way. You can want it, need it, and beg for it, but people don't own something they haven't contributed to. Human nature doesn't work that way. This applies to a room full of 7 year olds or a room full of 50-somethings. Participation is foundational to the process, but for whatever reason people are resistant to building in that participation. It could be fear, or intimidation, or laziness, but the process you use matters. Pay attention to how you engage staff, support people to put something IN, and notice how incredible it is to experience the magic that comes with individual and collective ownership. As a leader, it doesn't get much better, or cooler, than this!

❷ Ownership

Action: Assessing Ownership

Describe what the current climate is around ownership with the team. Is there a difference around individual ownership, and collective ownership? Where is it working, and where could it be improved?

Define: What

What do you want to do to support increased ownership? What situations or circumstances (meetings, supervision, training etc.) could benefit from increased Input from the team?

- What is your specific, concrete and measurable goal? (How much, how many, by when?)
- What would having this mean for you, or do for you?
- What is of value to you about that goal?
- What does your goal look like when you've reached it, or how will you know you have reached it?

Clarify: Why

Why is it important for you to increase the individual and/or collective ownership of the team?

- Why does this matter to you?
- Why are you invested in reaching your goal?
- Why do you feel a sense of passion, commitment or alignment around this goal?
- Why is this goal a priority for you?
- Why would reaching this goal be of value to you, your work, your life?

Implement: How

How will you take action to consistently build in opportunities for people to have Input?

- How will you start this initiative, and how will you involve or include others?
- How will you develop a plan and timeline for reaching this goal?
- How will you know you have achieved your goal?
- How will you address any barriers, challenges or obstacles?
- How/to whom will you be accountable?

③ Clear on Conflict

"There is nothing more stressful to me than conflict. I know people look to me to handle things, but to be honest I really hate it and will do absolutely anything to avoid it." –Team Leader

"When there are issues amongst staff my first inclination is to deny anything is wrong and hope that it disappears!" –Coordinator

"Conflict makes me nervous. I'm not sure what to do and I'm scared if I get involved I could make things worse." –Associate Director

The final area of focus around being professional is dedicated to what you do when things get hard, or challenging, or don't go as you had hoped, planned or expected. As a leader, how do you handle conflict? Under your leadership, what kind of environment are people working in? Is it one where conflict brews over time, eroding relationships and trust, until things become intolerable and something big happens? Is the environment a breeding ground for denial, avoidance, resentment, anger and distrust? Is conflict the unspoken plague keeping you awake at night as it systematically eats away at the foundation of your team, department or group?

Or, is conflict actually viewed nothing more than a simple difference of opinion, which is acknowledged, embraced, and in some ways celebrated because it reflected engagement, participation, passion and investment? Can you even imagine how incredible that kind of climate would be, for staff and for leaders? How would that paradigm shift serve to redefine this very scary word and deflate it back down to the essence of what it really is, which is simply a difference of opinions?

Conflict is a scary concept because people have had such upsetting, unhealthy, and dysfunctional experiences with what it means, what it represents, what it does, and what it creates. Generally speaking, the people you are in charge of leading and inspiring are not coming to work every day with extensive lifetimes experiences and histories full of healthy and respectful strategies to handle conflict. Many times in training we will talk about how people do the best they can, based on what they have, which is especially important to remember with conflict. It's not like people are saving their best moves, and most evolved strategies, tools, and approaches to life. They aren't holding back the good stuff with their conflict resolution skills; you are getting the best they have to give.

This is an important topic in professional arenas because the stress, fear, and anxiety people associate with conflict is going to be just as present in a work situation as it would be in their personal lives. If you are a leader/supervisor know you will inevitably be in a position to deal with, handle, and address conflict within a team. As you may already know, things can go to a bad place very fast, and this is certainly not an issue that a leader can successfully hide from or ignore. It's important you become adept at handling conflict. It would be even better if you could go beyond "handling it" and develop the remarkable skill to acknowledge, embrace, and celebrate any time there is a difference of opinions with the team.

When people have proudly shared they do not experience conflict at work it's actually quite concerning because a lack of conflict is often an indication people don't care or they have disengaged. If people are disconnected, or feel they have no position, no value, or no voice, they say very little. When people shut down and stop talking or sharing opinions there is a natural reduction in contrary opinions. This is not something for a leader to be proud of, as it is an indication of how much things have deteriorated with a team. As a leader, it is up to you to pay attention to the atmosphere of participation you are creating and maintaining. It is going to be on you to help redefine the meaning of conflict within your team, but know your efforts will have tremendous benefit.

In your efforts to shift the concept of conflict, it requires you explore what conflict means to you. If you are like most people this isn't a benign topic. What if you stepped away from your present framework on conflict and you explored a new angle? What if you embraced a whole new paradigm on what conflict represents? What if your new position contained an inherently positive paradigm of what conflict means, and what conflict can do? Try this angle on and see what you think...

A New Understanding on Conflict

Conflict is a powerful testament to a dynamic, talented and vibrant team. Conflict means:

1 People care enough about the situation to have an opinion.

2 People care enough about the situation to take a position.

3 People care enough about the situation to be invested in the outcome.

As a leader, all three of those are viewed as positives with the capacity to contribute to the team, the work, and the overall mission/vision of your agency, program, or business. Remember, you are modeling how to redefine conflict and showing people what it looks like when you are not scared of it, you don't run from it, and you don't deny it. You are showing people what can happen when you acknowledge, embrace, and celebrate it!

As a leader, you can be swimming in this new perspective, and you might even be making progress with how the team is interpreting and experiencing conflict, but that won't help you with concrete strategies to work through it when it actually happens on the team. As the leader, how do you successfully support people to move through diverse opinions, insights, perspectives, beliefs, or positions, and reach the shared goal beyond their differences?

Celebrating conflict isn't going to resolve it, so what can you do? You give people the skills and tools to work through it successfully, starting with the Conflict GPS model below.

Conflict GPS: Directions to Resolve Conflict

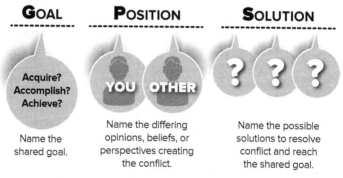

Goal
Acquire?
Accomplish?
Achieve?

Name the shared goal.

Position
YOU OTHER

Name the differing opinions, beliefs, or perspectives creating the conflict.

Solution
? ? ?

Name the possible solutions to resolve conflict and reach the shared goal.

©2015 Say Yes Institutue

This easy to use, easy to remember model was created to provide teams with a common language and shared tool to move through their differences of opinion. This linear process has been used with countless teams and it works because the three components are concrete, clear, and help people navigate conflict without deteriorating to an emotionally-charged split of a "winner/loser." Here are the three steps:

GOAL: It is of foundational importance for people to shape conflict resolution by first defining their shared goal. Conflict often serves as a catalyst to instantly position people in an automatic adversarial or competitive position. This happens because people forget, or overlook, the fact that they actually have a shared goal. It's often helpful for groups to start with a "same shirts, same team" approach to help people remember they are actually on the same side, with a shared goal. They are not enemies, competitors, or rivals. The first step typically helps shift and reframe the energy and deflates the high emotions that quickly surface whenever a real or perceived conflict emerges.

It is worth mentioning sometimes there is an interesting variable which is uncovered at the first step; the people who are in conflict actually do not have a shared goal. This lack of an overlap means, from the outset, they are not in the same conversation, which means there is no chance for resolving it. The first step of naming the goal will illuminate any fundamental "miss" in communication or understanding around the root of the conflict. If that "miss" is not addressed the parties will be in for a long and futile exchange with no chance for resolution because at the core they do not have a shared goal.

POSITION: The next step, after ensuring and establishing a shared goal, is to have people name the positions they have taken. This isn't about proving you are right and the other person is wrong, it is to illustrate there are many different paths to reaching resolution. For many people conflict brings up very strong feelings, interrupting one's ability to acknowledge other possibilities, positions, or perspectives. Taking time and making space to name the differing positions is a powerful way to review possible options. Again it is a helpful reminder for people to keep revisiting the philosophy of, "same shirts, same team." There are always different options and opinions on how to achieve a goal, but when both people remember they have a vested interest in reaching the goal it helps keep emotions in check. When people remain calm, engaged, and invested, they stay connected to the process as they explore different perspectives and possibilities. This step will illustrate both parties have a vested interest in reaching the goal but the possible path there is different. They are not enemies, they are not fighting, they merely have a difference of opinion on achieving the end game.

SOLUTION: The final step is focused on identifying possible solutions to resolve or rectify the differences. If there is an agreed upon shared goal, and a clear understanding of the different positions, there will be a greater likelihood of openness to exploring solutions. When people are at the point of naming a range of different solutions they are often ready to compromise as they identify the action needed to reach the shared goal. Typically by the end of the conversation people are feeling connected to the shared goal, heard by the other person and in a positive position to reach some level of resolution around their difference of opinions. The final solution is often a combination of ideas from both parties, or an entirely new idea generated by the conversations from the GPS model.

Currently the concept of conflict may have a negative connotation; as a leader you play a pivotal role in helping people expand their understanding around what conflict can mean. As a leader you are modeling and teaching how the team could effectively and successfully navigate differences of opinion. Being professional comes with a lot of expectations around how you will gracefully handle workplace situations, but as you know there needs to be extra attention paid to how you handle challenges. For most leaders conflict is typically the biggest challenge they will face at work.

As a leader you are committed to fostering an actively engaged team, with all members sharing ideas, suggestions, insights, experiences, and opinions. Because of your commitment to active participation, you are invested in maintaining a professional work environment with the capacity to consistently embrace and support effective, healthy, and successful conflict resolution.

Action: Assessing Conflict

Currently, how to you handle and/or respond to conflict? Take an inventory of what it means to you, and how your experiences and beliefs about conflict with conflict impacts the team. What do you do when it happens? How do you handle it? What do you say?

Define: What

What would it look like if you redefined conflict and held a more positive perception of what it means to have a difference of opinions in the workplace?

- What is your specific, concrete and measurable goal? (How much, how many, by when?)
- What would having this mean for you, or do for you?
- What is of value to you about that goal?
- What does your goal look like when you've reached it, or how will you know you have reached it?

Clarify: Why

Why are you committed to expanding your comfort with conflict? Why does this matter? Why will this be beneficial to your team?

- Why are you invested in reaching your goal?
- Why do you feel a sense of passion, commitment or alignment around this goal?
- Why is this goal a priority for you?
- Why would reaching this goal be of value to you, your work, your life?

Implement: How

How will you be a leader around reframing conflict? How will you take action on this initiative, as you work to shift the current perception of what conflict is and what it means?

- How will you develop a plan and timeline for reaching this goal?
- How will you know you have achieved your goal?
- How will you address any barriers, challenges or obstacles?
- How/to whom will you be accountable?

> *The person who knows
> how will always have
> a job. The person who
> knows why will always be
> his boss.*
>
> –ALANIS MORISSETTE

7

You're new at this...

Special Focus: New Supervisors, Managers, and Leaders

This final chapter gives an extra highlight to supervisors/managers/leaders just out of the gates and new to being accountable for other people. It's important to note being "new" to the field of supervising does not necessarily correlate to one's chronological age. Some are new to supervising at 25 years old, while others are new to it at 53 years old. This section is for those beginning the journey and interested in a few more tips, thoughts, and suggestions on how to be successful in this new phase of leadership.

Out of the Gates: *Powerful*

You're new at this...

Trust you have the capacity to lead. This is one of the biggest pieces new supervisors struggle with and in the absence of this trust, they are hesitant, uncertain, or overwhelmed, making it hard to move through the days feeling powerful.

▧ Understand confidence does not automatically accompany your new job title, so dig deep and find it. On days you don't feel it, dig deeper. It's on you to find it and feel it.

▧ Unless your family owns the company, chances are you got this position because the hiring team believed you were the best person for the job and have the education, experience, and capacity to succeed. Believe them—then prove them right.

- Get clear on what you are bringing to this position. The world doesn't keep a running list of all of your impressive qualifications, or everything fabulous about you, so you better keep it. You are great at a lot of things, and you have a lot to offer. Your capacity to be viewed as powerful, and capable of leading a team, hinges on your ability to believe it.

- People aren't going to adore you, follow you, or respect you for your title. People adore, follow, and respect people who are solid, clear, consistent, and focused.

- You do not know all you need to know, and this will not be an effortless transition, but you can do it. There will be ongoing gaps in what you know, and although you may encounter a significant learning curve, remember it is possible to simultaneously hold what know, with what you have yet to learn. You may not have all the details of the job, the team, or the work that is being done, but you do have the education, experience, capacity, foundation, skills, etc. to support this team to greatness. You will make mistakes, you will miss the mark, you will have gaps and that's ok. You may not have it all figured out yet, but know in time, you will.

- Being "new" will be what they see initially, but people quickly move beyond that if you are moving forward. If you're stuck on being "new" then the team will be stuck too.

- You know being powerful isn't about power over someone else. Because you are new you will diligently and tirelessly work to build powerful, positive, and professional relationships with the team, as you model investment, respect, and hard work.

- You authentically show up, consistently offering the best you have. You become more powerful as you grow and learn, owning your skills/strengths while supporting others to do the same.

Being powerful takes a little getting used to, but you've got this one.

"Is there anything you want to remember and/or add about being Powerful?"

Out of the Gates: *Positive*

You're new at this...

You understand people don't always love their jobs, or the business/agency they work for, and they aren't all going to adore their bosses or the leadership in charge. As the leader, what are you going to do with that? Are you joining them? You will need to decide how you are going to move through your days if/when the office culture leans to the negative side. You don't need to lead daily workshops on being positive, or conduct hourly cheers in the office around motivation and morale, but you do need to decide on a daily basis how you are going to handle your approach to work and the people on your team.

░ You are dialed in to the fact not all offices filled with positive people, in a positive culture, focused on looking for what is right, what is working and what is going well. You recognize there are negative environments, unhealthy dynamics, and toxic people out there. What does this mean for a new supervisor? A lot. There are countless examples of "good" people going "bad" in "bad" environments. If people aren't paying attention this shift can happen quickly, quietly, and under the radar. Be clear on where you stand, intentional in your focus/energy, and regularly check in to make sure you're outlook/perspective is where you want it to be. (Be aware the reverse is also true and people who have been toxic or negative in "bad" environments can become positive and engaged team players in a "good" climate/culture!)

- You understand you can be positive, even when others aren't, or can't, or won't. You are new at this but you model how to be excited, optimistic, invested in the possibility/potential of what can be and not hyper-focused on what's flawed, broken, or missing.

- Your positive energy can inspire and motivate others, and you use that power on a daily basis to benefit the team and the work you are doing together.

- You realize it's not your job to make other people be positive; you can only control how you move through this world. There are people out there 34 years, 56 years, or 68 years deep in to living life finding everything wrong, everywhere they go, and they're certainly not going to change because of you. The key, especially for a leader, is to not let someone else's negative journey hijack your positive approach to work or to life!

- Even though you may not have tons of experience, you already know being negative erodes your credibility, your power, your impact, your success, and your capacity to enjoy all parts of life, including work.

- You understand how you move through the world has far reaching ripple effects so when you choose where your focus will be you choose wisely and you lean to the positive side of things. You know this position is giving you the opportunity to lay an amazing foundation to build your reputation, and your career on, and you're going to take full advantage of it.

Being positive inspires people, making you a bona-fide "people magnet"—which is magical when you're the leader!

"Is there anything you want to remember and/or add about being Positive?"

Out of the Gates: *Professional*
You're new at this...

Being an example or a model for the right way to do things isn't always easy or effortless, but it matters and it's worth it, so you will put in the daily effort to do it.

▨ You understand every day isn't going to be amazing, and every interaction, meeting, supervision, evaluation etc., isn't going to embody perfection. Sometimes you will make hard decisions, and many times you will be challenged. People aren't always going to like you, approve of your decisions, or support your actions. Remember to trust yourself when things aren't easy, because difficulties don't necessarily mean you are doing it wrong. Being professional means you are doing the hard stuff with grace, clarity, integrity, consistency, and a sense of fairness.

▨ Maya Angelou said, "I've learned that people will forget what you said, people will forget what you did, but people will never forget how you made them feel." As a leader, it is on your to ensure your team feels respected, valued, appreciated, and supported. Your investment on the positive, and commitment to recognizing the value and contribution of each member of the team, translates to a phenomenal platform of loyalty, investment, and high caliber work!

You have friends, and they are all people you can not and do not have the capacity to write up, reprimand, promote, or pay. You actually have a lot of friends, and every day you head in to work remembering although you may really like the people around you, they are not your friends. You consistently maintain healthy and professional boundaries with the team. Partying, drinking, relationships, over-sharing and disclosures around trauma/drama in your personal life are categorized in your "what not to do as a supervisor" list! Your personal life may not always be neat or orderly and that's ok because life isn't an endless array of Kodak moments. Sometimes life can be a big mess with a lot that can and will go wrong, just make sure the people helping you clean up the "mess" are your equals; your friends, your family, or your peers. The biggest landmine for new supervisors tends to be struggles with boundaries. Never let your professional image, reputation, or credibility be diminished, damaged, or destroyed by struggles in your personal life. Once people know, they will always know and remember. And, most importantly, what people remember, they share. One time, one night, one bad decision has done a lot of damage to many supervisors. Learn from them and keep your boundaries clear, tight, and consistent.

You are the supervisor today, but what would happen if, in the future, you found yourself in a different role or position with someone you used to supervise? Imagine you, or someone in your life, interviewing for a job and the person making the final decision was someone from your team today. Would that be a horrific nightmare, or an unexpected delight? It's happens, perhaps more than you would think. When you are professional it means you will be able to cross paths, directly or indirectly, in any context, at any point in the future, and it would be a pleasant surprise. Being professional ensures a level of respect and appreciation capable of transcending your current roles/positions and qualifies you as a leader people will always remember fondly; a powerful, positive, professional leader.

Being professional isn't a quality that comes with a title; it happens whenever someone is looked to as an example for how to do it right. You're new at this, but you are confident you will be that example.

"Is there anything you want to remember and/or add about being Professional?"

Just show up.
Be brave.
Be kind.
Rest.
Try again.

-Glennon Doyle Melton

8

Top Ten:
Big Questions, Big Answers

A s a wrap-up I wanted to share some of the questions I have been asked countless times over the years, as well as some of the most common comments I have heard at trainings/workshops and keynotes. Here are the top ten questions & comments...

❶ My boss needs to be here—not me. There is nothing I can do with this because I'm not in charge. What am I supposed to do?
There are so many versions of this one, but they all center around people looking for permission to not have to own any of this because it's somebody else's problem. People want to tell me they aren't "the one" that should be there, and they aren't "the one" that needs this. The truth is they are probably right, the boss probably would benefit from being there, but the boss isn't there. You know who else isn't there? Your significant other, your coworker, your sister-in-law, neighbor, the new receptionist at your doctor's office, or your son. I have heard they should all be at the training too. My standard reply is something like, "I hear you, but that person isn't here, you are! Focus on what you can do with this, within your own life, right now." These skills/tools are not just about work, they are about how you move through life and all people can benefit from help in dealing with all of the people we encounter in life.
* It is always interesting to note that most of the people who "didn't need to be there" because they weren't the boss, will come up at the end and

share what they learned, or where they will use the information. It's a little bit of validation that what we cover is relevant and timely for all people, regardless of title or whether they want to be there or not!

❷ What if you just don't like someone? What do you do about that?

You don't have to like everyone. I actually would be surprised, and alarmed, if you did. Some people you will love and wish you could spend the rest of your life on an island with them. But then there is the rest of the world. Those people who for you feels like the equivalent of chewing tinfoil. It's a given you aren't going to like everyone—but it actually doesn't matter who you like or don't like. People skills are not about liking people, they are about how you handle yourself, regardless of how you feel. People need to show up and treat others with respect, and kindness, and compassion. Find the positive whenever possible, and when you do find it, say something about it. At the end of the day, and at the end of our lives, nobody will ever say they regret being positive, or kind, or they wish they were less compassionate.

My goal in this work is to support people to consistently move through this world in the best way they can, and that often involves our relationships with other people. This is an easy one: We need to stop fixating on who we don't like, and start focusing on how we treat people. The better equipped we are to do that, the better all of our lives will be.

❸ Your positive approach won't work for me.

When people proudly proclaim this I think my response often surprises them. I tell them, "You are absolutely right." For a moment they are filled with glee because they have proven to the wacky, positive lady there's something out there that cannot be shifted or reframed to make it sparkly and pretty. But the glee is only momentary, because then I follow with this, "You are right because you have taken a position and your position is, 'this can't/won't work because of_____.'" You took a position and all you will do now is seek evidence to support that position. At the end of every day you will succeed in building your case and will prove you are right. And you will be right; you are right not because that's how this person/situation or is, you are right because you only sought out evidence to support your case. That is the only evidence you looked for, focused on, and held on to." At this point the glee has faded and they are befuddled. The confusion is due to the tragic reality that most people I encounter have never, ever, ever been in a position where they were encouraged to explore the possibility they were not reporting on life as impartial observers. There is nothing even remotely impartial about how this is going down. In my experience most people are in a frenzy—diligently proving their negative position on a range of topics in their daily lives which serves to do nothing more than cause perpetual agitation.

Bottom line on this one: If you are consistently agitated, frustrated, stressed, angry, or exhausted then you are probably busy taking negative positions on people/situations/events. If you like that feeling and it's working for you, keep doing it. If you don't, change it and check out what some positive positions can do for you. You may find you're more relaxed, at peace, have more energy, and you're significantly happier. Not a bad way to live, is it? Try it.

❹ What do you do when the people around you (family, friends, coworkers/boss) are not positive? How do you stay positive when the people around you aren't?

Great news—you have no control over anyone else. If Myrtle wants to go through life miserable she can and there is absolutely nothing you can do about it. Nothing.

I don't care how much you want someone to be different, or how much better you think life could be if s/he would just lean in to the positive side of life and see that not everything in the world is wrong, you don't get a vote. You can beg, plead, cry, scream, threaten, lecture, and sulk but at the end of the day you have done nothing except wasted your energy. You would be much better off using your precious and finite energy to move through the world focused on how you can find the positive in your days. When you do that you will obviously benefit, but you also model for others what it looks like—and how great it feels!

❺ How can I get _____ (fill in the blank—a friend, spouse, boss, coworker, kid, neighbor, elected official, clerk at a store...) to be happier/positive?

Ready for this one?

Here it is: You can't.

Let it go. Give it up. Forget it.

I don't care how much you want someone to be happier or come to a training and join the Positive Posse, it's not happening.

I cannot tell you how many people have come up to me to excitedly ask how they can head out and go share this great news about happy/ positive strategies with someone in their life who is angry, bitter, negative, toxic, resentful, or miserable because they want to...ready for this... CHANGE THEM. They want to know how they can take this person out of the land of gloom and doom and put them in the rainbows and ponies and ice cream cones. I admire their optimism, but I feel like I have a professional responsibility to help them let the dream die before they walk in to a painful dose of reality. This isn't how any of this works.

This is about you. Just you. Why? Because you cannot change, fix, save, or heal someone else. You are in charge of you.

You.

Only you. The focus and the foundation is you. The only thing you can control or change, is you. People push back against this in the biggest way because they feel like there must be a way to reach someone you care about and make things different for that person. This doesn't mean you don't impact other people, because you absolutely do. You can model for people what it look like to move through life with a positive lens, and by sharing that you can serve to inspire others—but you can't change them. So, take that one off your "to do" list. I can definitively say it's not going to happen.

❻ I'm busy and although I get what you're saying about the well activity, I just don't have time to take care of myself.

I get it. You're super busy, you're really important, and all the people need you. You have lots of places you need to get to and lots of things you need to do. You have balls in the air you must catch, and appointments and meetings and events. You volunteer, and coach, and conduct, and lead, and organize things for people. I so get it and I really do hear you. But here is the deal, at some point you're going to run out and burn out. It's just how this equation works. You cannot give what you don't have. I have said this countless times and I will keep saying it. This is one of the hardest things for people to grasp, so it remains one of the foundational pieces of what I talk about. I have had people come up to me after keynotes, tears running down their faces, sharing how much they wished they had heard this years ago. They talk about how desperately they needed to be reminded that they don't have to do it all, or be it all. They share story after story of not really understanding all of this works around self-care until a health crisis forced them to take notice of how overextended they were. My hope is we can notice this before this a diagnosis or health scare, because it doesn't have to get to that. I get that you're busy, but you need to get that you don't have time to not take care of you—because your body can only operate being overextended for so long before something gives. We don't need to be stubborn with this one—let's listen carefully and respond early. (Plus, the up-side to all of this is for all of you Type A people is, the better you take care of you then the more you have to give and the more you can do! What a win/win!)

❼ I get what you're saying, and I'm on board right now, but then I am going back out there where this is going to fade away and I'm going fall right back to where I was. How do I stay in this place and keep using these tools?

This is a tough one for people because this is not a "flip the switch" kind of process. You don't just become different, or shift your perspective and arrive at the land of the happy people. This is a daily choice, and an ongoing process. There is no finish line, no trophy, and no special club you suddenly become part of. There is no trick to this and it is just about as unglamorous as you can get. You literally wake up every day and decide what you are going to look for in your day and all of the people in it. Every day, all day, you make choices and you take positions on everything and everybody. Your life is all of those choices and positions strung together—and some will go the positive route, while others go with the negative. Either way, it's your choice.

People will tell me after the first part of a training they leave feeling inspired and like they have all of this positive energy they can't wait to unleash on the world. Then I come back for part two of a training and it's like a sitcom version of a group confession of sorts. People tell me they left with great intentions and they applied the skills/tools for a few days, or few weeks, but then "daily life" just sucked the life right out of them and they lost it and stopped. They feel disappointed in themselves and like they failed.

The conversation which follows centers around how to maintain momentum, and explores how this is not a "one and done" kind of thing. This is an approach to moving through the world, and it's a fluid process.

For example, when you are taking care of yourself (Filling the Well) you will have the capacity to give more to people and find the positive in situations. When you are drained, you become increasingly negative. It isn't tricky to connect the dots on this one. You can't give what you don't have, and many want to believe if you're in the positive club you will stay there. In perpetuity. That's not the case. Every day is it's own little journey—and every interaction is a chance to make a choice around how you will approach the situation or the person.

The amazing news is, you absolutely can "get it" and understand it, and immediately apply it successfully. You can have an off day, a negative interaction, or a less than exemplary display of a mood—and you aren't out of the club! We are all trying, every day, to do the best we can in how we approach things. An "off day" (or as one woman said as she was confessing how negative she had been since I had seen her last, an "off season") doesn't mean it's over for you. It means you're aware the negative isn't how you want to do things and you get the chance to choose another approach. Every meeting, every conversation, every day you get that chance. Take it.

❽ Some people are just smiley, happy, Pollyanna, "sun is always shining" kinds of people and I'm not like that. This isn't me.

Good one! In the interest of transparency I will tell you this: I'm not one of those people either. The belief there are just simple people out there who wake up happy and somehow miss the pervasive misery in the world which the rest of us are acutely dialed in to, is a myth. Positive people are not always happy. They are not always skipping through meadows of flowers, in awe of the beauty and magnificence of the world. Those "sun is always shining" folks are merely people who are able to simultaneously recognize that while there certainly is a lot wrong in the world, there still is still a whole lot right—and they choose to shine the spotlight on those moments. Those moments where people are amazing, and kind, and good, and generous, and compassionate. They choose to notice and share the "wow" parts of life, and not the moments of agitation. Every day people (even the happy ones) are subject to the full range of emotions we can experience as humans and they choose to resist the seductive whirl of the negative.

There is a quote which circulates on Facebook over and over which says, "Feelings are much like waves. We can't stop them from coming, but we can choose which one to surf." Whether by default, or by choice, there are many people who can't jump on a miserable wave fast enough—but that doesn't mean there aren't a whole lot of positive waves out there. The most powerful conversations with people are often centered on people recognizing, for the first time, the role they play in how they experience the world.

I can't tell people how to move through the world because I don't get a vote in their lives and their approach to how the choose to live it. The only thing I can do in my role is to keep showing up and asking people over and over, "Is this working for you?" If they say yes, and they dig the negativity and misery they spend their days with, then that's fine and they can continue holding membership to the "hate everyone and hate everything" club. If their approach isn't working for them, and they would like to actually like daily life a little more, and enjoy the people in their lives a little more, that can happen. Developing a perspective, or choosing what lens you look through, is an active (daily!) process and you control the outcome. If that hasn't been you or your approach in the past, it doesn't mean it can't be you. You get to decide how you experience your life, and although I know I still don't get a vote, if I did I would vote that you find and feel the positive a whole lot more!

❾ Are you always happy?

This one always makes me laugh. Not at all. I think I can be positive, and I am wildly addicted to naming the positive wherever/whenever possible, but nobody is "always" anything. I love to share with people that The Positive Promise is my absolute favorite model and I really apply that a lot in my life. To the point where people in my life have said, "Are you kidding? We really have to find the manager again? Seriously?" And I'm like, "Yeah, we really do. Again."

But as much as I can find the positive, I am not a Pollyanna who believes all is well and it will all work out. I hold the positive, but I also simultaneously hold the hard & heartbreaking parts of life too. I can get lost in pieces of life that don't make sense and hurt too much to understand how there can be anything beyond the pain. But I have incredible people in my life and on days when I forget, or I can't find it, they remind me and they can make me laugh. I could not do this work, or this whole life journey thing, if I didn't have such amazing people with me.

This is why I now ask people at every training/keynote this question:

Do you have someone in your life who can make you laugh when it feels like nothing is funny? Someone who you feel so grateful to have in your world and you do not know how you could do it without them? Someone who gets you, is there for you, and who can help you get through something when you can't see the other side?" When people start nodding, smiling, and putting their hands up, I ask the next question. And it's a big one. I ask them, "Can you call that person today and thank them? Can you call them and say this may sound wacky for just a regular Tuesday night, but you wanted to just tell them you are so lucky/grateful/off-the-grid happy that you get to have them in your life? Can you do that?" And this is where things get incredibly cool.

People say they will do it. And then, they really do. People are actually doing this and the results are amazing! They are the stuff chills, tears, and immense gratitude are made of! I have gotten incredible feedback from people about what has happened when they have picked up that phone, or gone to lunch/dinner, and told someone what they mean to them and how much it matters that they get to have this person on this life journey. People have been so gracious sharing their experiences and have called, emailed, and sent messages through LinkedIn and Facebook. As I read them, tears streaming down my face, I keep thinking, "This. This is what it's all about." Because it is.

⑩ You seem like you really love your work.

Being told after a training or a keynote that people felt like I really love what I do is one of the greatest compliments I could ever get because it's true, and I am thrilled people can feel that. When I am talking to a group I want to share every bit of information I have that could be useful to them. My goal when I am done is that I have (hopefully!) given them something concrete they can take away to do/use/try/apply. I feel grateful I get to spend my time focusing on how people move through life—personally and professionally.

I have been asked many times about what is the most powerful part of this work, and it is hearing back from people about what clicked for them, whether it is immediately after a training, or years later. I value the experiences people share with me about how they were able to apply skills/tools and strategies in their lives and the results they got from trying something new. I love what I do because it is direct, real, immediate and can be applied personally and professionally.

I think about moments which were so amazing I remember thinking, "If my world ended right now then it was a good run!." I won't list them all, because as someone who pays attention to the positive there are many, but one was after a keynote when a banquet staff member waited in a line of people let me know that she had heard hundreds of keynotes but had never heard anything like this because she felt like I was talking directly to her. She said she was so excited to use what she had heard within her life, starting with her daughter, and she thanked me for being there that day because she said I had no idea how much she needed that. It was all I could do to hold back the tears—because it felt like everything I had ever done, or tried to do, was sitting in that moment.

Another moment happened in a group for parents who were dealing with a lot of struggles (homelessness, addiction/recovery, mental health issues, domestic violence) and at the end of the group I asked, "What will you remember, do, try, or use from tonight's group?" A young woman raised her hand and in an explicative-filled testimonial I experienced one of my proudest moments ever. (You can insert your own colorful language and fill-in-the-blanks here.) What she said sounded like this, "You have no____idea how many _____groups I have been to in my _____life because I have been in groups since I was _____11 years old. I have never learned a _____thing and I can't believe how much as I just_____ learned in this one_____group. I hope you keep doing what you're doing because you're _____good and people need to_____hear this _____stuff."

So yes—it doesn't get better than that.

It is safe to say I beyond love what I do.

The game of life is the game of boomerangs. Our thoughts, deeds and words return to us sooner or later, with astounding accuracy.

–Florence Shinn

Closing

The bottom line of it all is this: It's all about people and perspective. At home, at work, in the world. We all know we can't control people, but we can control how we view them and what we look for. The more positive we are in our approach to the world, and the people in it, the better our lives will be. Promise.

Whatever your role or title may be, at home or at work, you most likely want to be successful. You want to inspire, motivate, support, encourage, and lead in a powerful and productive way. You want to do the best job possible, for you and for the people around you. You deserve to have the skills and tools to enjoy the people that you are leading, managing, working with, or living with.

This is a final reminder you are impacting people in a powerful way, and you want to make sure that impact will be positive. You have the capacity to teach, support and inspire the people around you. You have the opportunity to model people skills and show others what it looks like when you show up and do it well. Give yourself credit for your commitment to building skills and trying on new angles to look at your work with people, because not everyone is willing to take on that kind of growth. Congratulations for your commitment, and your effort. It will make a difference, to you and to all fortunate enough to cross paths with you!

In closing, here are a few parting words for you which I had started in response to a question I was asked once at a training about any observations/tips I had gathered over the years about what could make people's lives better. Here is a summary of what *I Wish People Knew*. Each little thought holds the power to create a seismic shift in how someone moves through the world and while some of these have been covered in the book, many are additional snippets gathered from years of working with people to build emotional intelligence skills. Here is one more opportunity to decide if anything clicks and helps you do some shifting, growing, or expanding.

I Wish People Knew

- Take care of yourself, because you can't give what you don't have. If you feel like you're running on empty, you are. Refill, refuel, replenish. Do it for you and for all the people in your world.

- You won't know if something works, or doesn't work, until you try it. As I've said to countless people over the years, "Clarity doesn't come from sitting on the couch!" At some point it's time to stop analyzing, stop assessing, stop thinking, and start doing.

- You will get more mileage out of taking a minute to think, "What is my goal in this situation?" than you will by any book, workshop, coaching, or training. In any situation, spending a few seconds to get clear on your goal will help shift and shape your energy, focus, and the plan for action. Being clear on your goal will tap in to your intrinsic strengths to adeptly handle any situation, even the hard ones.

- People respond to your energy, so make sure you are putting out what you want to get back.

- Saying "thank you" benefits everyone, but in reality it actually does more for you than for the person you're saying it to. Look for ways every day to say it, a lot.

- Progress isn't a neat, straight, linear process. It doesn't always follow your plan, and sometimes doesn't even acknowledge you even had a plan. Many times you won't know you're even making it until you look back and see it.

▓ "Sleeping on it" certainly can help settle your thoughts, but some people seem to live on bed rest. Contemplation, analysis, and speculation have a lot of people living life on pause.

▓ Fear isn't a deal breaker. Remind yourself often that fear is a positive thing, because if you are scared because it means you're about to do something new. It will work, and that's great, or it won't, and you'll get feedback about what to do differently next time. Either way, you win.

▓ If you are scared and want to move through it, name the worst case scenario and see if you could live through it. If you could, then you do it. If you couldn't, then maybe that's a risk you aren't in a position to take. It's a miraculous cure for our irrational fears! (FYI: In my coaching, nobody has ever said that they couldn't live through a "worst case scenario" result of a risk they were contemplating.)

▓ Focusing on the positive will always take you to a better place, and the transport is almost instantaneous.

▓ Along those lines, being positive means people will like you and want to be around you. At home, at work, and in the world, people really like to be around positive people.
*Footnote: "People like to be around positive people" may not be universally applicable to exceptionally miserable, negative, or toxic people. If you are too positive you become a repellent for them and they want to stay away—which isn't necessarily a bad thing.

▓ The quality of your life is all about your relationships, at home, at work, and in the world. Be the kind of person people want to be around.

▓ For you, and the people you work with, work is one part of life. It's a significant part, but it is not the only part. A balanced life is "macro," which means you can see and hold all parts, and you find the pleasure that comes from the perspective of the bigger picture. An unbalanced life is "micro," focused on what is wrong, and typically manifests as stress, despair, and anxiety. Remember, if you feel overwhelmed, stressed, or like you're stuck in a really negative place, somehow you have lost perspective and balance. Pick your head up and expand what you are seeing. The bigger picture doesn't take away what's wrong, but it reminds you there is still a lot right.

- Just because you've done it one way for as long as you can remember, it doesn't mean there isn't another way. You are always growing, evolving, learning and expanding. Life continuously presents opportunities to try on different strategies/approaches/tools to help in your journey, so take advantage of that and use them!

- Taking five minutes to just sit and take a breath, alone, could make all the difference in your day. This is especially crucial on those days you feel like you absolutely do not have the five minutes to spare.

- Finally, find the humor in life. There is a whole lot there, if you choose to see it.

Please know I would love to hear questions, thoughts, or feedback at:

www.sayyesinstitute.com
https://www.facebook.com/SayYesInstitute

About Carrie Stack

Carrie Stack, M.Ed. is the founder of the Say Yes Institute, providing training and coaching around personal and professional development. She has had the privilege of working with thousands of people across the country to build emotional intelligence skills using concrete and transferable skills/tools. She is also the author of *Conversations with the Future*, co-founder of EO Your Life, and the founder of Courage2Know.

Carrie Stack, M.Ed.
Certified Life Coach, Author, Trainer
Say Yes Institute
121 Loring Ave.
Suite 250
Salem, MA 01970

www.sayyesinstitute.com
www.facebook.com/sayyesinstitute

Made in the USA
Charleston, SC
14 April 2015